For the Sake of America II

Sheila Holm

Deeper Truth, Ancient & Current Roots
Revealed for Repentance to Result in
Flow of Restoration, A Flood of Blessings
For The Sake Of America!

For the Sake of America II

For the Sake of America II

ISBN-10: 548452424
ISBN-13: 978-1548452421

Unless otherwise indicated all scriptures are taken from the
New King James version of the Bible.

http://hisbest4us.org

Facebook: HISBest4us, Sheila Holm Christian Author

Printed in USA by HIS Best Publishing

DEDICATION

To my Mom who is 95 and to my Dad (who went home to be with Our Father at 93 on November 5, 2011; a deep man of GOD who shared prophetic words at key points during my lifetime and especially during our last conversation twelve days before he passed away. GOD revealed truth to him because he shared GOD's truth when he said all I had experienced would result in the truth being revealed to the people, soon, very soon. I trusted it would be my restoration. I had no idea it would become the restoration plan for our nation) for everything Our Father has revealed to me will matter to the believers who operate in faith.

To Gene and LaVonne McGee who have stood by me during the depths of the details and prayed through with me 'no matter what' while my *faith walk* continues.

To Bishop McKinney for standing firm in prayer with me since the day we met in 2000. For the deep prophetic word spoken over me that day and for providing the Foreword for the trilogy of books released in 2014: ***It's A Faith Walk, GOD's Storehouse Principle*** (book & workbook) and ***GOD's Currency,*** books which I trusted would be the only books released since the truth is: IF GOD's people who are called by His name, II Chronicles 7:14, would be filled with faith, learning how to function within His storehouse then GOD's currency would be evident and flow among the believers within the body of Christ and it would not matter what the world does because GOD's people would not be affected!

To Rebecca King for providing the truth about the glory for the truth is: ***Christ gave us the glory before He went to the cross, so we would be one as He and the Father are one.*** **John 17:22.**

To Heather Rock for standing firm in truth, for remaining strong within the lineage of the Mississippians, for sharing The Apocrypha and enjoying the journey with our LORD.

To Dorothy Spaulding for immediately hearing the deeper truth, for scheduling multiple TV interviews so the believers can begin to comprehend the glory Our Father has 'in store' for all who love Him, **I Corinthians 2:9**, and for making the connections with Perry Stone, Dr Sandra Kennedy and Barbara Houseman the moment ***For The Sake Of America*** was released.

To Rodney Howard-Browne for your willingness to share the deeper truth no matter who is in the midst of the multitude for the truth must be revealed so all believers can repent and restoration of our lives and our nation can flow like a mighty flood.

To Bill Morford for remaining obedient until the ***One New Man Bible Revealing Jewish Roots and Power*** was translated direct from the Hebrew and made available to all Christians so believers will see and know the truth: ***We are no longer Gentiles, and we are not to do as the Gentiles do!*** For providing the book ***Fulfillment of Prophecy*** by Eliezer Ben-Yehuda for our Father revealed the truth to him: ***The two things without which the Jews will not be a nation: The Land and the Language.*** Critical stand

4

he took for the believers because America is back in the position of not protecting the blessed land GOD provided or the language!

To all Native Americans, all who were 'on the land and operating under Divine Law', especially the lost tribes of Israel who have known the truth about the blessed nation known as America for centuries; a deeper truth which was not openly revealed to the current generations.

To Rodney Howard-Browne for remaining strong while sharing the deeper truth within each meeting and especially in the midst of your amazing humor, especially while confirming you are now one of the few actual, official African-American citizens.

To Nancy Cheek for sharing *For The Sake Of America* with Dr. Neigel Bigpond and Reverend Clifton Pettit which led to the beginning days of the deeper truth journey regarding the roots affecting America to this day and for joining with Sherry Point in prayer about all of it. Grateful for your prayers and for insisting I would not be leaving Georgia before I have a time of rest in Branson, Missouri. Everything about the trip became the major pivot point in my journey. GOD's timing is impeccable!

To Marty and Lynn Burson for knowing 'it has something to do with the Brownsville Revival', for confirming the timing and the fact Our Father was preparing a person in San Diego, California (1992 forward; exactly aligning with all our Father has done to prepare for for 'Assignment Georgia' in these days) and that He would send them at the appointed time, a person who they would know as soon as they met because the person would already be setting off fires all over Georgia. GOD sent me to specific regions as revealed within *For The Sake Of America* which confirmed Georgia has been GOD's focus; He sent me to all regions while showing me the same vision as 'setting off hand grenades vs. fires'. The confirmation facts and hand motions Marty shared were very specific!

To Denise Wilson-El who told me so many facts 'beyond human comprehension' about the lost tribes of Israel being in America, about 'being home' and not coming from Africa and so much more. For sharing facts confirmed by many of GOD's sources within days of your willingness to introduce me to the deeper truth about the Native people in America, I am grateful!

To Elizabeth 'Liz' Judd for hearing the details and immediately comprehending the truth, for merely walking to her bookcase and handing me the book which a non-believing Archaeologist wrote after our Father proved Jesus Christ walked the land. The Native Americans knew His as the *LORD of wind and water*, knew of only one man *who spoke a thousand languages, healed the sick, raised the dead, and taught in the same words as Jesus Himself.*

To Deborah Hosey for hearing GOD's voice and praying through with me during these amazing days in Augusta, Georgia so the deeper truth about the significance of Georgia could be revealed & shared with believers who have eyes to see & ears to hear the truth. For introducing me to Healing Springs the first morning, and so much more including her interest and excitement in each layer of GOD's truth and His reveal of the 'flow' within hours, the flow He promised to me after He promised the flow in Georgia which would spread across America to the prophets *For The Sake Of America*.

To Clesie Ann Adams who has taken on each fact shared, researched the truth and printed the facts to share with those who will see and hear the truth and share it far & wide!

To Aaron Cohrs for sharing David Barton's *Original Intent, America's Godly Heritage,* and for so much more, especially for following the prompting of our LORD to identify a specific scripture 'as America', a fact which is revealed within this book.

To the many who have strengthened me the past 27 years, to those who have challenged me, hosted me, helped to secure assets in California & Georgia while I am traveling: Paul, Lisa & Debbie.

To Tommy and Penelope Wilson for praying while sitting behind me at Blackville Church of GOD and for saying, *What GOD has revealed to you needs to be in a book. Believers need to know the truth.* The title to the second book happened the same way, on the only day when I returned to visit the church in June, 2017.

To Bruce and Ruth Mosher for your interest in every phase of the journey, and to Paula Mosher Wallace for donating the car in Georgia which made travel possible to each region in Georgia.

To Michael and Denita Turner for opening your home to host me when I was at the point of leaving Georgia for good the third time, for arranging opportunities to share the truth with believers in the region, for providing peace and protection which is required to complete upon the assignment. The truth within *For The Sake Of America* would not be in print if I had left Georgia as I planned.

To each one who walked in faith, believing, while the LORD has taken me to each nation in preparation for Georgia after directing specific items to pack in one suitcase plus the instruction to 'bring the lap top' for a three week trip to Macon in 2013!

To Kirk Cameron for all of the effort to produce and distribute the film *Monumental,* for providing the truth about the Pilgrims, the Faith Monument, how America became a blessed nation with liberty and freedom for all, and for the research by David Barton, so all believers in America will be reminded of the truth!

To all citizens who are believers in the only one true living LORD who will stand firm in these days to take back what the enemy stole from our lives, States and America, especially to the Pilgrims who sacrificed all so the truth would be brought to America and become available to all who seek the word, the truth. To the mighty men and women of the LORD who persevered through all situations even becoming martyrs so the bible would be translated into English (Tyndale; DVD title, *GOD's Outlaw*).

To my family and friends for praying through and standing firm with me during these unique days in HIStory!

Table of Contents

Introduction

Body of Christ, *What were we thinking?*

There are ancient roots which are linked to current roots. They are roots which we have not repented for or dealt with so we can be free!

Dealing with what we see 'on the surface' does not resolve anything because the roots have to be dealt with. To do this, we have to know the deeper truth.

The deeper truth reveals what we have done to operate against the plan our Father has for us while we are 'on planet Earth'. As each layer is revealed, I trust you will be ready to ask the same question I have been asking, *What were we thinking?*

We are ALL made in the image of our Father, our LORD GOD. However, we operate with each other as though we are not.

What were we thinking?

We are ALL of various shades of skin color, eye color, physical shapes and unique historical backgrounds while we are ALL formed in His image, sent by Him to be here and live our lives representing Him.

A very special book was given to me as a gift from Bill & Gwen Morford. *Fulfillment of Prophecy, The Life Story of Eliezer Ben-Yehuda 1858-1922.* Ben Yehuda was given a short life span prediction by a doctor. He immediately devoted the remainder of his days to study and teach Hebrew and the truth. His life was extended many years. His famous quote, *The two things without which the Jews will not be a nation: The Land and the Language.*

We have not retained our language.

The lost tribes of Israel traveled here; retained their language.

We have not known the truth about our land or our language.

What were we thinking?

We are 'grafted in' once we claim our salvation in Christ, our Messiah, Yeshua Hamashiach. Therefore, we are no longer Gentiles and we are not to do what the Gentiles do. However, we continue doing as the Gentiles do without question.

What were we thinking?

We were to 'possess until He comes'.

What were we thinking?

Without full knowledge, we have compromised with the world, passed on information without knowing if it was true or not, and we became comfortable in 'how it is' in these days.

What were we thinking?

As a body of believers across America:

1. We 'stayed out of politics' and now we wonder, *What happened?*

What were we thinking?

2. Pilgrims brought the truth and set forth upon a 500 year plan. For 250 years all was aligned and all lived in peace. Then, everything changed to a world based plan. We 'trained up the next generations to be successful in the world'. We supported all youth in obtaining a world based education to 'do as the world does' vs. training each generation to hear the voice of the only true living LORD, our Father who art in heaven and now we wonder, *What happened to the youth who are supposed to be highly educated due to being on our college campuses?*

What were we thinking?

3. We are in a nation where we were 'free to worship' while the church remains separated from the state 'on purpose' so we do not have a monarch or president who can tell us how we can worship, where we can worship and what we can believe. However, we have let the government control the church! *What happened?*

What were we thinking?

Current roots require repentance!

Within *For The Sake Of America* many of the 'current roots' were identified.

People are amazed about the facts while it has not become a lightning bolt experience which motivates us to repent for where we are or what happened to cause us to get here from the place our Father prepared for us.

More prayer was required.

Our Father immediately directed my attention to truth we did not even know existed!

Deeper truth which has shaken me to my very core. I trust it will do the same to you when you realize the depth of the current roots which link directly to the ancient roots.

We are embarking on an adventure, together. You can trust I will be here, standing with you while you and your family gather together and pray, repent and seek the next step.

Ancient roots require repentance!

The ancient roots have been covered over by lies for so long, it was not easy to 'take it all in' the first time it was shared with me.

However, our Father is patient and He has remained close to me and shown me the deeper truth we did not know that we did not

14

even know! Many confirmations have been provided during the journey into the deeper truth.

It is absolutely worth the process for the truth is absolutely what sets us, the captives, free!

Praying with and for you and your family while you take on this amazing journey with me for it has truly been more like a treasure hunt.

The good news is, GOD provides the treasure and to Him we are the treasure!

The depth of the truth is so profound, our Father has done everything to make it as simple as possible for us to realize we did not know what was 'so wrong' that our America would be this far 'off course' in these days.

The LORD confirmed significant truth about America within *For The Sake Of America.* GOD provided the truth about our history. He confirmed the exact facts to Gary Kah which confirm school text books are not revealing the truth about our history.

Since *For The Sake Of America was released,* each time I have tried to leave (aka, escape from) Georgia our Father shares another fact about the deeper truth!

There is so much for us to comprehend.

So much truth was hidden from us for so long, covered up with lies which have caused us to proceed within the lies due to being encased in a web of deceit.

We were lulled.

We became comfortable.

We actually reached a point within the body of believers that we wanted everything to 'be OK, covered by GOD's grace'.

Only our Father can reveal all of the truth to us in such a way to cause us to stand in awe and in faith, fully participating in repenting for all our Father reveals to us.

Bottom Line: There is so much we need to repent for so we can be restored to His truth for it is His heart's desire for us to know what is true and base our choices and our words shared upon His truth and stop accepting and acting upon what the world states as truth.

Nothing about this book has been easy for me to express.

So much was such a shock, I am grateful the South has a term which confirms how amazed I am with the root facts our Father has shared with me:

Have you ever heard such?

Have you ever seen such?

I'll let you guess how many times I've used these phrases within this amazing journey.

Repentance is not a typical message shared within the body of Christ. How often do we repent, personally? When we do, is it only focused upon me and mine?

Me and mine are fine became the status resulting in the complete destruction of Sodom and Gomorrah. People often say 'it was all about lust and sex' but, it was not. It was due to the lack of concern for truth and for others. GOD's plan was ignored. The people followed their plan and became comfortable 'in the world'. They did what they wanted to do.

For more than 20 years, I have sought the help of top leaders in the body of Christ to focus upon waking up the believers within the body to the fact America has become a Sodom and Gomorrah. The cities of Sodom and Gomorrah were in the land of Canaan near the Dead Sea.

They leadership responded with the facts about the end times and the decline of America has to do with the end times and nobody can change the events of the end times.

What were we thinking?

When you have a moment to review the scripture, it will confirm that Lot was not even able to convince his two son-in-laws to leave after the angel told them, *Tonight is the night so you must depart!*

Are we listening to the warnings?

It is time! It is our shift on planet Earth!

You may want to buckle your seat belt for the facts our Father has revealed to me as the ancient roots, the deeper truth!

If we do not repent personally. If the majority of people do not repent in a region. What is the option for us to have a future for our nation?

If the angel warned us go tonight, would we be prepared?

GOD's plan: It was always about *Feed My Lambs, Especially My Widows and Orphans and beyond all the gifts we have, Love.*

GOD made it clear within the scriptures.

Have we focused upon taking care of the widows and orphans in our family? In our region? In our nation?

GOD has a big plan for each of us and His plan is for us to live abundantly and prosper!

II Chronicles 7:14. *If My people who are called by My name will humble themselves, and pray and seek My face, and turn from their wicked ways* (REPENT), *then I will hear from heaven, and will forgive their sin and heal their land* (RESTORE).

We are each 'a hunk of dust'. When we repent, we will be restored. Families will be restored when they repent. When we gather and repent with believers in our region and our state, our region and state will be restored. When the body of Christ gathers together in unity, aligns and repents across the nation, America will be restored.

This was the promise of our Father to me, when the vision and word *For The Sake Of America* after the facts were passed on to me from the representatives of the prophets, a process which became an assignment after the word was shared from Bob Jones by Kin Clark during a wedding reception in May of 2015.

When we repent for the atrocities, we will see the flow of blessings in Georgia and on to South and North Carolina.

Then, when the believers across the nation align in repentance prayers GOD's promise within the vision and word will be fulfilled.

Then, the blessings of our LORD will continue to flow across America 'like a mighty flood'.

Our Father has proven His deeper truth within this journey which He wants me to reveal to you now for His promise to us is true: *Eye has not seen nor ear heard nor can the mind begin to conceive the glory our Father has 'in store' for those who love Him.* **1 Corinthians 2:9.**

To live from glory to glory, it is important to comprehend that our Savior, the Messiah, confirmed in **John 17:22** that He gave us the glory that we would be one as He and the Father are one, while He was with us!

Praying we will stop saying we give our Father back the glory for He wants us to have the glory, to live in the glory and from glory to glory so we might unite together as ONE BODY, living life abundantly and prospering as our soul prospers. It's all confirmed within the scriptures!

What is our purpose, our destiny?

What will fill our days for the rest of our lives?

Take as much time as you want to think about your answer! I will ask you the same question at the end of this book.

GOD has a better plan.

An amazing, treasure hunt awaits while we journey together with Him into the glory realm where He reveals the deeper truth!

LORD we are grateful Your hand is upon us, Your truth is being revealed to us while You provide the option for us to repent so we will, our families will, our fellowships, regions and states will, and our America will be restored!

Chapter 1   For the Sake of America II

If you have not reviewed the Introduction, please read it now. Do not worry, I will be waiting for you right here when you have completed reading it and you will not miss out on anything regarding the mystery and treasure hunt within this book.

Our Father is preparing us, so we can travel with Him through the most amazing historical journey into the deeper truth, a journey our Father has designed as though it is a lifetime Treasure Hunt!

Our Father who art in Heaven has a great sense of humor!

Here I am with Him preparing a second book about the significance of Georgia to America.

This was not going to happen, or so I thought.

That's right, due to four books and a devotional the LORD provided to me in great detail being set aside to complete *For The Sake Of America,* October 2016, according to 'my human understanding' a second book would not be released about the significance of Georgia to America in these days.

After *For The Sake Of America* was released so many people asked, *Why is Georgia so important?*

Our Father immediately confirmed *'it is in the scriptures'.*

In the scriptures? It was a funny moment because even though I often remind the LORD I'm not a bible scholar, I actually told our Father I did not remember seeing Georgia within the scriptures.

Without hesitation, our Father confirmed: *The last shall be first and the first, last.* **Matthew 19:30 and 20:16.**

Georgia was the last Colony and the structure was established by the Native Americans and the Pilgrims. The Pilgrims received all of the credit even though the Pilgrims operated in the truth based upon the complete bible (portion in the 1611 bible was removed in the mid-1800's) and in peace with the Native Americans. The LORD was starting to reveal a deeper level of understanding before He directed my path 'back in time' to realize who the true Native Americans were.

End of the Beginning

The song by David Phelps, a member of the Gaither Vocal Band for many years, has impacted everything on this journey.

Since they say hindsight gives us 20/20 vision, and it is easier to see what GOD is doing while looking back and realizing how much He has done and how much deep truth He has provided, I stand in awe as I begin to reveal His orchestration at the end phase of this journey. Then, we will swing right back to this moment in time for Chapter 2 of this book. Exciting since these details are about GOD's flow, as He promised, at the *'End of the Beginning'*.

Where is the Flow?

Our Father promised the prophets 'a flow which will spread across Georgia, through North and South Carolina, and then across America like a mighty flood'. To me, a flow was not evident so a second book was not 'timely'.

GOD knew it was time and He confirmed the urgency so, I cried out to see a flow vs. a trickle here and there since that is all I was seeing in each region our LORD placed my feet throughout Georgia. Then, I went into deep rest with Him.

Early the next morning, GOD provided three confirmations within an hour. This is so much like Him and how He operates.

Number 1 message received:

I'm sure since you are still in Georgia, you are aware of the flow of oil from a bible.

Great to know there is a flow GOD but, it would be great to know where!

Number 2 message received:

Since you are still in Georgia, I trust you are hearing about the flow of oil from a bible in North Georgia.

Great to know it is in a region of Georgia dear GOD but, a specific clue regarding the location would be helpful.

Number 3 message received from a Facebook article sent within a private message from a friend in Georgia the moment she received it from her friend in North Carolina:

(Town name and the type of retail store were specifically identified.)

Thanking GOD for the clues while I started calling the stores!

It was a bit of a shock to realize the other stores were so close to the amazing miracle of GOD, the store where the flow was evident and yet, they knew absolutely nothing about the flow of oil from a bible.

After calling the initial list, I asked GOD for help and He directed me to the exact store within the same moment. It is so great to have GOD with me as a 'partner with wisdom, sharing truth while I progress through this process'.

The employee offered for me to attend a weekly prayer meeting on Tuesday mornings from 10-12 noon. Since I was being hosted more than four hours from the store, not including rush hour traffic in Atlanta, I was hopeful another option would be offered.

There I was, busy sharing details with the employee regarding my request to know about a flow but, she did not provide a different response.

The LORD gently offered an option, *Tell her about the Brownsville Revival ...*

I was not aware of the fact the employee was making notes and the store owner was looking at the notes over her shoulder during our conversation but, GOD knew the next step to take in the conversation when He gently asked me the second time, *Please tell her about the Brownsville Revival.*

Important for you to know I was not being easy with GOD in this moment.

In fact, without realizing it, I was actually giving GOD a geography lesson about Brownsville being located below South Georgia and the oil is located in North Georgia (about 25 miles south of the Tennessee border) before I realized GOD was more aware of the geography of Georgia than I was on that day, as of today or I will ever be at any time in the future!

I've not been to Brownsville and I did not attend the Revival. However, the beginning of the 'how and why I returned to Georgia after a short visit to Nebraska to be with my Mom' (with only GOD & mom being aware of the fact I planned on leaving Georgia) is directly related to the word delivered by a Brownsville Revival Prophet, shared within Chapter 2.

The moment the employee wrote the note 'Brownsville Revival', the owner of the store grabbed the phone. We talked briefly. Within 10 minutes, my car was loaded and I was on the freeway for the journey toward the north border of Georgia!

Flow of oil: Exactly one week after President Trump was inaugurated, the beads of oil which were forming on the wall of the prayer room in the shop began appearing on the pages of the bible.

The flow began when the bible was opened to Psalms 39. It continued to flow through the words on each page until it reached the end of the concordance. Then, it began at the beginning of the bible and continued to flow through Psalms 38.

The LORD wanted the oil to be kept and not wasted, so the bible was placed in a zip lock bag. Within a short time, it filled the bag. So, the bible was placed in a bigger and bigger container until they realized it needed to be placed in a large plastic storage bin type of container.

Flow of oil direct from the word.
Consistent flow, day and night.
Flow began on Friday, January 27, 2017.

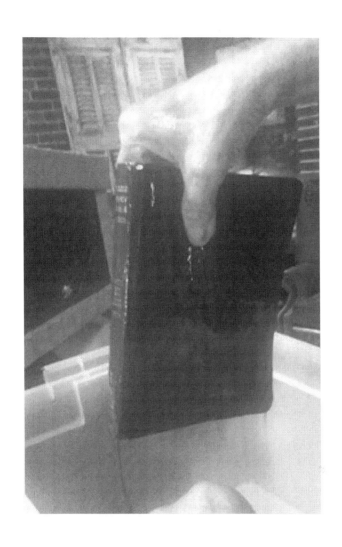

Steady flow for six months before my visit.

No words are blurred.

Highlighting has not faded.

Every Monday evening the fellowship in the region, comprised of believers within various local churches, gathers together to fill vials with the oil flow of the week. Then, the team of about 25 people assist with the prayer meetings on Tuesday mornings from 10 and 12 noon and beyond, until all receive prayer. The team prays together and for the people who attend the prayer meetings. Sometimes over 200 people attend the Tuesday morning prayer meeting due to the word of the testimonies reaching other regions.

It was a gift to be able to witness many healings in the very moment of the healing prayers. One example: A woman was dealing with arthritis in her hands and wrist. The moment she placed her hand in the oil, evidence of the addition of arthritis to the bones disappeared and her hand returned to normal.

Whitfield. The owner of the store shared amazing details about Whitfield. I am not from Georgia so I did not realize the impact of Whitfield as an evangelist from England or that the county which borders Tennessee is Whitfield county. So much was happening and so many facts, it was hard to 'take it all in' during the moments in North Georgia.

Sharing Truth at Whole Life Ministries
Augusta, Georgia

Impossible to keep this information to myself, so I shared the details with a staff member of Dr. Sandra Kennedy's Whole Life Ministry in Augusta, Georgia by text and email on Wednesday.

We did not have a moment to talk about the details before she made copies for each of the ministry staff members.

When the Thursday evening service began, Dr. Kennedy asked me to come forward and share the facts about the flow of oil.

After sharing a few key details, I walked to the back of the chapel (location for the Monday and Thursday evening services) to help the crew insert the photos within their computer system to show the flow of oil on the screens at the front of the chapel.

Dr. Kennedy immediately noticed beads of the oil appearing on the wood at the altar, directly behind where I was standing while I was sharing the facts with the people.

It was a surprise since I did not touch the wood and I did not have an oil vial with me nor did I have any of the oil on my hands.

When I walked back to the front of the chapel, I touched the beads and they were definitely the same oil. The beads appeared independent of each other and each one expanded exactly as they did on the wall of the prayer room in the store in North Georgia.

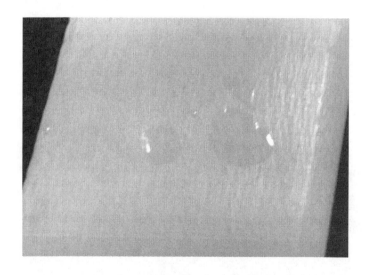

Dr. Kennedy invited all of the people to come forward and witness the oil. Nearly all of the people lined up within the center aisle and walked forward to the front of the chapel. Some of the people were not able to resist touching the oil with a finger. Each one who touched the oil noticed the expansion of the oil when it bubbled and continued to flow on their hand.

Whitfield: Dr. Kennedy shared a few details about her great-great grandmother establishing churches in Georgia in the time of Whitfield. In fact, she was the one who brought Whitfield to Georgia from England.

A woman who received a vial from me placed a speck upon the palm of her hand. The oil continued to expand forming a pond in the middle of her hand. Then, it began to follow along the lines in her palm until it reached the side of her hand.

Since she heard the word the LORD shared with the people in the shop that the oil is not to be wasted, she placed her other hand against the side of her palm and a pond immediately formed in the palm of her other hand.

All who touched the oil and the woman with the pond in both of her hands came forward. The people formed a line in the center aisle of the chapel once again. Each one touched the oil and it bubbled and expanded on their hands. The oil on the wood continued to bead and expand throughout the evening service.

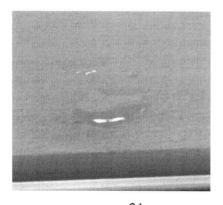

The presence of our LORD is how and why the oil appears.

It is an oil. It is odorless and colorless. It is not an oil structure chemically known to man, per a thorough lab analysis, and yet, it is proven to clearly be an oil.

Testimonies

The healing testimonies from the people experiencing healing prayers with the oil shared for specific healing are absolutely miraculous!

A woman called and told her neighbor about the oil that night. The neighbor asked if she could come over in her pajamas because she wanted prayer for a brain tumor so large it could not be dealt with. The next day the neighbor went to her doctor and asked for the same test to be conducted.

Results: Doctor reported, *Tumor turned to dust so there is no brain tumor to be dealt with!*

An uncle asked for a vial to share with his sister because his nephew is an Uber driver and he was shot in the hip. Doctors were saying it would be a year of specific rehab before a surgery could be performed to remove the bullet. It took a week for the vial to arrive in Tampa, Florida. The man's sister took the vial to the hospital the same night and prayed with her son.

Results: The next day, doctors performed another test. They were shocked. The bullet became 'dislodged' from the hip and moved to a position just under the surface of the skin 'on it's own'. The doctors came to the hospital room and removed the bullet, without surgery, while the young man remained in his hospital bed. He was released from the hospital within two to three days.

A woman asked for prayer due to a tick bite and red ant bites which she received while trying to deal with the tick bite! Her foot was so swollen it was nearly unrecognizable as a foot. Infection was evident from the tick bite on the foot, through her entire foot, ankle and it was starting to expand up her leg.

Results: The moment a drop of the oil was placed on her foot, the oil 'raced across her entire foot, ankle and leg'. It appeared the oil was racing to the end of the spread of the infection to capture the infection and bring it back out of her body at the location of the tick bite. In that moment, all pain and swelling of the foot disappeared. The woman was in such awe of what she witnessed, she did not even realize all evidence of the red ant bites completely disappeared from her foot at the exact same time.

A woman asked her boyfriend to attend a meeting about the oil. He received a COPD diagnosis, his feet and legs were swollen and he was on an oxygen tank. The sanctuary was full so they sat in the overflow room.

Results: At the end of the meeting, the moment they entered the sanctuary for prayer, before prayer or anointing in oil, the swelling disappeared and he did not need the oxygen tank any more that evening or since that evening! Praise GOD!

There are so many testimonies, I could insert the awesome miracles of our LORD for many pages. However, the depth of truth our LORD revealed is what resulted in providing the evidence of the flow, beginning in Georgia.

Therefore, now that are aware of the flow once we repent and enter into the presence of our LORD I am going to take you on the adventurous journey from the very newest *'End of the Beginning'* orchestrated and revealed by our Father!

Chapter 2   Significance of GOD's Plan for America

As soon as *For The Sake Of America* was released, I trusted my assignment was complete in Georgia and therefore my next assignment would be revealed to me soon very soon.

GOD is so good. My hostess, Denita, knew it was merely the *End of the Beginning* with the book being promoted once it was in print. She was right! I was merely confirming my thoughts to myself while GOD knew I was squarely sitting at the very starting line of our Father's plan to reveal ancient roots, a deeper truth hidden from us for multiple centuries and generations!

Some people may say, *Shorten the book and just give us the facts.* However, those people would miss the depth of the journey due to not realizing our Father knows we are humans living an earthly experience 'in the natural' and He provides the depth of truth at the speed we can 'take it all in'.

Therefore, to avoid serious heart issues which would result from taking in so much truth we did not even realize we did not know, our Father graciously chooses to walk me through each layer of truth step by step 'for my sake'. Then, He guides me while He helps me put the details into the same format He orchestrated for me so you can enjoy the 'ah ha' moments each time He reveals another 'gem', aka, a deeper layer of truth.

Therefore, again, I am going to walk you through the 'deeper truth' our Father has revealed to me. It's a lot to take in after the truth He revealed within *For The Sake Of America* opened our eyes and ears to His truth for us. Grateful our Father keeps His hand upon us while we are continuing our journey with Him, aka, our personal Faith Walk on planet Earth!

Our Father has continued to put emphasis upon the 'urgency' while revealing each of the many layers of the 'deeper truth' step by step. He did not want me to begin to reveal a specific topic due to His prompting that a deeper truth was known, a truth which I was not aware of at the time *For The Sake Of America* was released. It was hard to comprehend at first.

Now, I realize His deeper truth would be a complete book 'on it's own' due to the truth not being revealed to our generations.

He has provided so many 'ah ha' moments since *For The Sake Of America* was released. He has divinely orchestrated mighty introductions and appointments and He confirmed the title and subtitle within a vision! Therefore, I surrendered! It is time to reveal the truth so we will know what we, as both the body of believers and as Americans, are dealing with due to the lack of knowledge. **Hosea 4:6** . *My people perish for lack of knowledge.* We need GOD's wisdom regarding specific areas of repentance of roots established within the ancient to current generations.

Each time a deeper truth is revealed, we will have a chance to repent individually, for our family, for our region and our America.

Be sure to take a deep breath with each 'ah ha' moment so you can enjoy the 'revealing of each layer of truth' as our Father has revealed it to me. Again, He is guiding this process so I can reveal the truth to you layer by layer, step by step.

Personally, it has been a series of 'deer in headlights' reactions for me with 'no words to express what GOD revealed' each time the deeper truth is revealed to me 'for the first time'.

Regardless, I'm deeply grateful His confirmations have been so powerful and immediate because each confirmation assures me what our Father is revealing is His truth vs. what the world has passed on to us, generation to generation, tradition or 'human understanding'. Critical to realize the difference since the scripture is true: *My people perish for lack of knowledge.* **Hosea 4:6.**

Our LORD has provided so much to me in the exact method He enjoys because of His love for me and for each and every one of us. It is truly His special gift, His way of blessing us 'in the moment'.

His added sense of humor makes the deep and often devastating reality of what the lies have become and what they have done to affect us, divide us, bring divisions to the point of hatred rising up vs. the Love of Christ. The lies have kept us from knowing 'the earth journey of our ancestors' which is what each generation fights to protect! We were supposed to pass His truth on generation to generation. *LORD help us!*

Our LORD has turned the awful truth into an amazing treasure hunt for His truth is: *We are His treasure!*

After *For The Sake Of America* Was Released

GOD began to reveal the next step in His plan the same day the book was released. I found out the feedback from the editors resulted in the publisher sending the first copy of *For The Sake Of America* to President Trump during the month prior to the election!

Feedback, after the *For The Sake Of America* TV interviews in Augusta, Georgia, on Club 36 included comments similar to those made by the editors. Praise GOD!

A bigger blessing was realized when this status did not change after the 2nd or 3rd or even the 7th TV interview regarding the book.

Feedback was identical from various parts of America and around the globe while it was most endearing to hear the comments from the people who have lived in Georgia 40, 50 or more years who thought I was a major historian.

In fact, they actually thought I majored in history in college or I taught history in college. Wow! GOD is so good!

When I confirmed all facts came from our Father, our Jehovah, they agreed with me that our Father is absolutely amazing!

LORD we repent! Forgive us for any words, dreams of visions you have given to us over time which we did not act upon or share with others as you prompted and guided.

This being said, the first few times I heard the comments from people who thought I was going to write a second book about the significance of Georgia to America, I still laughed.

Trusting the research and history details were complete, I was ready for my next assignment and I trusted it was not going to be 'within Georgia'. Again, I was wrong.

GOD clearly planned on a second book when He told me to not reveal any details about the specific topic of slavery or segregation even though He confirmed He sent me to Georgia (2013) exactly 100 years after President Woodrow Wilson became President (1913). Wilson reinstated segregation in America within a list of devastating steps which were taken against We The People and our blessed nation of America within a few days of his inauguration.

GOD Sent Daniel

The first interview on Channel 49, Club 36 in Augusta Georgia resulted in an amazing presentation. A man, Daniel, was 'on task' during a typical busy day when GOD prompted him to turn on the TV. As soon as he heard a portion of my interview, the LORD prompted him to drive to the station.

We were leaving for lunch when Daniel arrived. It was clear he wanted to talk to me and it appeared it was something urgent! We did not have any time to talk at the studio so the founder and hostess of the program, Dorothy Spaulding, invited Daniel to join us for lunch.

We were going to a specific restaurant.

During the journey, while I was following Dorothy to a new location, it seemed like her plan changed. When Dorothy realized the problem, she prepared to call Daniel but, she merely had to take the call because he was already calling her!

When he arrived, he asked me to 'walk outside'.

Since Dorothy knew the man, I walked outside with him.

He pulled out his wallet and I could see a large circle which was 'wearing through' his leather wallet.

He began describing a special coin as he placed a Special Forces coin in my hand. In that moment, GOD was confirming to me that Daniel is going to give me the coin. I answered GOD out loud, *I'm not going to receive this coin.*

Daniel smiled and said, *No, I'm not going to give you my coin, I'm merely explaining what the coin represents. When we return from a mission, we line up for inspection. As the General proceeds down the line to shake our hands, he does a 'palm pass' of the coin to the hero of the mission.*

Daniel received a Special Forces coin and it was an amazing design. I was speechless in this moment.

Daniel continued to explain the process while confirming it was GOD's plan on this day, *As soon as I turned on the interview, GOD told me to get to the station and give you the coin. GOD designed the coin. He told me to keep it in my wallet until He confirms to me who I am to present to coin to.*

Front and Back of the Hero's Coin

Wow. Acknowledged by GOD. Hero's coin received. Trusting assignment is complete. Trusting GOD smiled because this moment in time was merely another *End of the Beginning.*

GOD became quite busy in the next few days and weeks sending people to me, people I did not know who spoke words which exactly confirmed why a second book was required.

I took it all back to GOD. I had a concern. Required?

While in prayer, the LORD revealed exactly why He was not allowing me to include slavery and segregation within *For The Sake Of America.* GOD knew We the People 'in order to form a more perfect union' need time to take in the depth of truth being revealed, and the time would be required before the deeper truth could be shared. Deeper truth?

GOD confirmed the deeper truth would be hard for me to take in. Wow. This phase would become a deep time of prayer and research to prepare for the follow-up book because GOD confirmed, *The facts will be unfamiliar.*

I was shocked. What could it be?

What is hidden from us about slavery and segregation?

It was an unfamiliar moment with our Father for me to hear about a 'deeper truth' which He could not reveal within *For The Sake Of America.*

I needed a time of restoring and refreshing!

Two nights with Rodney Howard-Brown, Tallahassee, Florida

Rare within America to hear the deep truth about America and how we have 'dropped the ball' as a body of Christ.

Deeply grateful for the truth shared each time I've heard Rodney in San Diego from the 1990's forward; in October 2015 in Thomasville, Georgia, witnessing evidence the people are waking up to the truth, and in June 2016 in Columbus, Georgia where Rodney shared an amazing testimony of another Daniel.

Daniel was attending seminary. He felt he needed to leave so he could do what GOD wanted him to do, say what GOD wanted him to say and go where GOD wanted him to go.

He wanted Rodney's counsel. His decision was already clear!

Immediately after Daniel left the seminary, the LORD asked him to buy a new bible and travel to Yemen.

Daniel was shocked GOD would send him to a Muslim country.

GOD merely reminded Daniel what he said he wanted to do because now, GOD was asking him to go.

Daniel bought the new bible, packed and flew to Yemen.

After he was settled in at the hotel, he prayed.

GOD merely gave him the address where the bible was to be delivered the next morning.

Daniel was shocked.

The address was in the Muslim section of Yemen!

GOD merely reminded Daniel of his request, his desire to go where GOD needed him to go. Daniel confirmed he would deliver the bible in the morning.

When Daniel arrived, he was a bit nervous while knocking on the door. A man answered and opened the door wide. The home was filled with people dressed in Muslim attire.

Daniel handed the bible to the man who was crying while he accepted the bible and said, ***Thank you Daniel.***

Daniel was shocked the man knew his name. When he asked the man how he knew his name, the man said, ***Jesus visited our home last night. He said He was sending His representative Daniel to bring us a bible so we can read it and know the truth.***

Rodney always lifts up, blesses and restores when he speaks because his messages are filled with the truth!

GOD directed my attention to Rodney's confirmation of becoming an American citizen which makes him one of the few, true African-Americans in America. GOD prompted me to hold on to this statement because it is part of the 'deeper truth'.

Refreshed and restored.

Ready to take on what GOD has laid out before me.

Knowing me and how much I question the facts and the status, our Father started sending confirming words from a lot of people who did not know me. A few, key examples:

1. Nancy Cheek, Chaplain for Dr. Neigel Bigpond and Reverend Clifton Pettit at the Native American Training Center attended the revelatory bible study of Rebecca King one month after the book was released. She purchased the book the minute she held a copy and prayed about it.

Nancy immediately shared information about the Native Americans being enslaved and their families being split apart and sold to other land owners in other areas up and down the coast of America, breaking families apart which resulted in the Native Americans losing the connections to their heritage and their lineage, etc.

This was 'new news' to me. This news became a major confirmation of a deeper truth which is revealed in greater detail as the journey into deeper truth unfolds chapter by chapter, beginning with **Chapter 3 Significance of Albany, Georgia to America.**

Nancy asked me to ship a copy of the book to both Dr. Neigel Bigpond and Reverend Pettit. Within a few days, after Nancy had extended invitations for each of them to come and visit her in Georgia for nearly two decades, Rev. Pettit, his wife and sister-in-law scheduled a trip. They drove to Georgia to speak to prayer partners within Nancy's home fellowship and to meet with me about the details our Father revealed regarding the location of the land per tribe and the stealing of land through fraudulent treaties, etc., etc., etc. **February 2017.**

Some facts were known. However, after Clifton left the room a few times during the 'time of meeting', I asked what was going on. He said that he was calling Mark.

I asked if everything was OK with Mark.

Clifton said he was leaving each time a new fact was revealed so he could call the mapper of the tribes, Mark, since the actions toward the Creek and their significant land areas were not known until he read the book and I confirmed GOD's guidance of the research process during the writing and editing phases. Blessed moments! Powerful to hear Clifton pray in the Cherokee language!

2. Contact with local Georgia State Senator, Blake Tillery, resulted in a return call the same day and a meeting within 24 hours. Georgia has not acknowledged the Trail of Tears or proceeded with Reconciliation. When I met Senator Tillery's assistant, Mandy Britt, GOD prompted me to give her a copy of *For The Sake Of America.* While she shared a few details about her family being 'full-blood Creek', the LORD prompted me to go to the car and bring back two more copies of *For The Sake Of America,* plus a copy of my *Nation Restoration & In Search of Wigglesworth* books.

When I re-entered the office, I told Mandy the LORD wanted me to give her my *In Search of Wigglesworth* book. She was surprised because she knew nothing about Wigglesworth. GOD is amazing! Early the next morning, Mandy was sending me text messages about Wigglesworth! GOD knew she used to operate in that level of faith and the book reminded her to walk in that level of faith in her life.

46

I confirmed GOD said *Nation Restoration* is for Senator Tillery. Then, I confirmed, *This is a copy of For The Sake Of America for Senator Tillery and yet, GOD prompted me to bring two copies.*

Before Mandy could answer, my host and Mandy started laughing. While I was outside, they were talking about Georgia State Senator Tillery sharing office space with Senator Williams. My host knew that both books, *Nation Restoration* and *For The Sake Of America* were with President Trump already and due to hearing about a connection with President Trump, he also shared the request I received to send a second copy of *For The Sake Of America* during the week prior to the inauguration due to the first copy being loaned to someone by President Trump.

Since I was not in the room for this conversation my only response was, *I have not met either Senator.*

My host and Mandy merely laughed, again, because they were inside the office talking about Senator Williams since he was the first State Senator in America (in fact, I believe he became the first State Representative) to back President Trump before Trump was the candidate. Senator Williams traveled on the campaign trail and became friends with Donald Trump long before Trump became the Republican candidate for President. **March 2017.**

3. Nancy Cheek invited me to her time share in Branson for a time of rest, April 1-10, so due to GOD confirming it was part of His plan for me to have a time of rest, I delayed my 'departure from Georgia plan' until the day after Branson.

It was going to be a special time of rest and prayer. However, due to Nancy's many connections, she arranged significant meetings with ministries in the region: Billye Brim, visits on two separate days for TV tapings with Jim Bakker, attendance during the Victory Conference with Kenneth Copeland and a Sunday service with Keith Moore, plus, GOD provided many confirmations! **April 2017.**

NOTE: While we were at the taping for Billye Brim she mentioned a connection between President Trump and the pastor of the Hebrides Revival. Immediately, our Father said that was not the right connection. Later that day, He prompted me to go back to the research of the Hebrides Revival which He directed during the writing of *It's A Faith Walk!* I remembered the video was long (a little more than one hour).

While I was hoping the LORD was not asking me to view it again, He directed my attention to the two women standing next to the pastor on the cover page of the You Tube video. I remembered the two women were Smith sisters. Then, GOD said, ***Google the genealogy of***

President Trump. I had no idea how to find out any facts about the genealogy of President Trump. Then, GOD merely stated what I needed to type in the search line on my lap top, *Genealogy of President Donald J Trump.*

Wow. It is merely a click on the name process to go back a few generations. President Trump was sworn in during his inauguration on his mother's bible, a fact he shared along with an endearing statement about his mother and that she was *"...a praying woman."*

Mother of President Donald Trump was Mary MacLeod nee Smith (her mother's maiden name was Smith; her mother's father was named Donald Smith; Grandmother of President Trump, Mary [Smith] MacLeod, born 1867 in the town of Stornoway).

When I clicked on the Smith side of the family, the father was named Donald.

NOTE: Middle name of Christ was used often for the oldest son or daughter in the families of that region, with the name pronounced more like the name Chris.

Middle name of Fred Trump, the older brother of President Donald Trump had the middle name of Christ.

The two Smith sisters, Peggy and Christine, were born within the same time frame and they were also from the small Isle of Lewis

They were living about 12 miles away in Barvas. The two sisters rarely left their home.

They were 84 and 82 in 1949 at the beginning of the Hebrides Revival which continued until 1953 and beyond in some parts of the Hebrides.

Peggy received the vision about the revival from our LORD. Peggy was blind.

Christine's body was full of arthritis.

Both sisters were fully healed during the Hebrides revival.

Amazing facts our LORD shares.

Grateful He helps with the research

Separate, Personal Note:

Family of President Donald J Trump is from Bavaria on his father's side and Scotland on his mother's side.

My mother's side of the family is the same. Her father's mother is from a family lineage in Bavaria and her father's father is from the Graham clan in Kilmarnock, Scotland.

In fact, my great-great grandfather James helped his uncle as a printer's assistant for the Kilmarnock Press when his uncle printed Robert Burns' 1851 Kilmarnock edition of his poems.

Branson was a deep, deep time of prayer through the night each and every night. Powerful days & nights!

Special detail: Lori Bakker's family is also Graham!

4. Sherry Point met me due to attending Rebecca King's weekly Revelatory Bible Study. Sherry arranged to be my hostess the night prior to the Branson trip and it became a special time of prayer to remain for the two nights upon my return from Branson.

    The first night was a time to begin the repacking phase and rest after the Branson journey. The night (until Midnight) was filled with deep prayer about the identical plan I come up with and share with our Father each time I think my time is complete and therefore I am focused upon how much to pack while praying: *IF there is a reason for me to stay, please confirm it or I will prepare to leave.*

I heard NOTHING from our Father during the day while I packed and loaded the car.

The second night, I trusted I needed to remain at the house and pray but, Sherry trusted I should attend a birthday party for a special boy turning six.

Immediately after I arrived, a couple (Marty & Lynn Burson) asked me about my ministry time in Georgia. Sherry confirmed, *There is a book.* They all laughed.

Sherry then cautioned them: *You will not want to put it down once you start reading it.* They wanted to know where they could obtain *For The Sake Of America.* I shared a few of the options while the LORD was prompting me to tell them I would leave both books with Sherry when I leave Georgia in the morning: *For The Sake Of America* and *It's A Faith Walk!*

It was my private agreement with the LORD which can become 'affected' if I tell people I am planning on leaving and I did not want a human plan, I wanted GOD's plan!

Sherry and the Burson's did not know I prayed about the identical plan I shared with our Father at each phase of the Georgia journey the night before the party. The LORD knew I was preparing to pack and go since I did not hear anything. Personally, I thought I knew that I knew I was leaving because it was clearly the '11th hour'.

GOD knew I would go to Nebraska and return to Georgia if a reason was presented in the next 24 hours or I would arrange to pack 'all of the stuff (stored in Macon, items gathered during more than three years 'in Georgia' during the winter, etc., and that means there is a good amount of stuff in the storage plus what was filling every inch of the car) and then leave Georgia' the next morning.

Marty & Lynn Burson are the founders of Millennial Kingdom Ministries in Albany, Georgia. They went into prayer immediately about the details they were hearing as they walked outside with the guests for the group photo.

Then, the LORD drew my attention to Marty while he was clearly 'in a conversation with the LORD' (aka, hands moving in strange directions while it was clear he was deep in a conversation without speaking a word out loud).

Marty turned and departed from the other people lining up for the photo. He walked back into the party room to ask me a question: *Where are you from?*

When I responded, *San Diego*, Marty confirmed, *That is what GOD said!*

Marty then sat down and shared a lot of details about Brownsville Revival. He talked about the Prophet who was reassuring the people the move of GOD would be going into Georgia and one by one the LORD was sending people to Albany. Then, when the Prophet returned to reassure the people: *Do not become weary,* and he stated again, *All is well because a person is being prepared in San Diego and they would know the person when they met them because they would already be 'setting off fires' throughout Georgia.*

Wow. This was a major GOD confirmation!

I did not attend Brownsville.

I only knew it happened near Pensacola, Florida.

However, the exact hand motion Marty used for 'setting off fires' is the exact hand motion our LORD used in a vision when He showed me that I was a person 'setting off hand grenades' for Him throughout Georgia!

Per GOD's direction, each time I told Him it was time for me to leave Georgia because 'they are not getting it', our Father kept confirming I was His ambassador and I was doing all He asked of me in each region of Georgia while the results were not my responsibility. Not responsible?

Shocked but, He knows me so well, if I do not see results I keep trying to help the people until they 'get it' and by doing that with each person I was slowing down the process or progress!

He reminded me exactly as He has reminded me many times of the day when I was four and I was marching in the meadow repeating: *They're really nice people but, they just don't get it!* At my current age, GOD was gently reminding me that I was only supposed to deliver His message by 'setting off hand grenades'. To do that, I had to stop being concerned about who gets the message, when they get the message or what they do about the message, or even whether they take action upon it or not. Doing what I see the Father do by saying what I hear the Father say and then departing, releasing it all back to Him! Christ made the process very clear. I just needed to be reminded!

The LORD encouraged me that night.

He knew I did not realize the significance of the words shared by Marty within the few moments we were at the party so He told me to research Brownsville.

Grateful everything was packed for my departure!

Research with our Father was intense!

Praying in Brownsville began in 1992, one prompting by the LORD of a series of promptings 25 years before 2017.

5. 25 years; Silver anniversary of GOD's Plan since 1992!

a) Prayers for Brownsville Revival began.

b) Marty was prompted to move; Atlanta to Albany.

c) GOD sent Graham Cooke to Macon to deliver a unity message to the leadership in the region.

d) Ministry man in Macon, prompted to move his family to Albany and to remain focused upon unity.

e) GOD lifted me up and out while the world started placing me on different ID as 'the answer' but, they repeatedly changed my ID and it quickly became a debacle which only operates in a downward spiral!

f) Leaders in the body of Christ moved to Albany.

Brownsville began in 1995.

The world insisted upon another ID change.

Promised it would be the last time.

1997/98, another change of ID. Enough!

GOD arranged for me to travel globally on 'His currency'.

Brownsville ended in 2000.

GOD returned me to America; focus upon America.

GOD re-established me with an auto, etc., in 2000.

When the men of GOD became weary by 2008, the Brownsville prophet reconfirmed the same word and assured them that GOD was preparing the person in San Diego.

Everything in my life changed by 2008.

Wow! GOD already knew I would go, 25 years ago!

Hindsight becomes more than 20/20 vision because it provides us with an amazing opportunity to see GOD's plan unfolding from His perspective while living life 'on planet earth' not focused upon seeking for earth to become as it is in heaven! GOD, forgive me!

Repentance for a LOT of '*all about me and operating according to my will stuff*' before I could close my eyes!

GOD confirmed I would only be leaving Georgia for a brief Nebraska visit of one to two weeks with my mom. He strengthened me to leave at 4 AM. Everyone who knows me clearly knows it was GOD who arranged this!

The nearly 20 hour journey only included a few moments 'off road' for gas tank stops every 300 miles. No stops to stretch or relax were required. Everyone who knows me clearly knows it was GOD who arranged this!

6. *For The Sake of America* was being shared across the nation and around the world, friend to friend. Prayer warriors in America and around the globe were confirming a second book about Georgia would be released regarding the deeper truth *For The Sake Of America*, before I shared anything about what our Father was sharing with me,

7. The confirmation from Marty that everything within my book aligned with what the LORD revealed to him was shared during a phone call and within an email a few days after I arrived in Nebraska. Marty's exact words encouraged me. Great to know everything was aligned, to know that GOD was orchestrating and that I had a plan from GOD which was confirmed: *I was going to pack the car and prepare to leave early May 1.*

Yikes!

An unusual rain, very unusual rain in the state of Nebraska, resulted in inches of rain falling in a short time period! I experienced this type of rain on a regular basis in Georgia. However, I grew up in Nebraska and nothing about the rain was like a Nebraska rain. In fact, the rain became heavier by sunset.

Therefore, my prayer with our Father confirmed that I was fully packed and ready to go at whatever hour He chose to wake me during the night to pack the car. I was ready to immediately load and leave.

Within moments, I shared this status with my mom. We said our good-byes even though she was going to get up before I left. Saying good-bye was for me, so she could rest knowing all is well.

8. Our Father has a special sense of humor!

When my eyes opened, the clock confirmed it was already daytime and GOD did not prompt me to do anything, yet.

Shocked.

When I asked what His plan was He merely said, *Look outside.*

Funny, GOD. The light confirms it is already daytime!

Important to realize, I did not mean to question or argue the point with our Father but, I already knew the sun was up and due to losing an hour on the from Central to East Coast time, the arrival time was going to be too late to leave for Georgia as promised.

Snow Storm on May 1, 2017
Only in this exact region in the Northeast Corner of Nebraska
Storm Left the local Weather Forecaster in Complete Shock

Weather Report:
Unusual Storm in Denver; Headed Straight for Kansas City
Changed Direction, Lifted up into the Atmosphere
A Weather Phenomenon

Today I realize, the weather report was truly funny.

The forecaster actually said it was an unusual phenomenon which occurred

The shift in the weather pattern happened exactly during the moments of my prayer with our Father! Wow. Funny.

Then, GOD prompted me to look up the definition of phenomenon because GOD said He prompted the forecaster to use that exact word (whether it was 'in the teleprompter or not').

Phenomenon: *A fact, an occurrence or circumstance observed to exist or happen, especially one whose cause or explanation is in question.*

Storm Direction and Plan Changed

Exact time of my Conversation with our LORD on Sunday

Snow ONLY Fell in a small part of the far
Northeast Corner of Nebraska
Six Inches in my Hometown, before Sunrise on Monday

Two Inches Recorded in a few Surrounding Towns
Tow Trucks Unable to Keep Up With Cars Sliding Off Roads
Schools and Businesses Closed

Shocked. Wow. Snowstorm in May? Six inches!

Shocked.

I made a promise to begin my return journey to Georgia on Monday morning, May 1.

More prayer required.

Before I received a response from the LORD or a call from Georgia, mom received a call from my brother Keith. He confirmed a flight plan to be with mom for mother's day weekend. Since we have not shared time together since our father's funeral in November, 2011, mom hoped I would be able to stay two more weeks.

More prayer required.

Within moments, I received the answer.

Marty & Lynn Burson sent a quick email. They confirmed the LORD prompted them during their morning prayer time to offer for me to extend my time with family and to have a time of rest with Him before I return to Georgia after Mother's day.

Wow. Fully aligned.

Before we shared the full details with each other, our LORD had already arranged the next steps for both of us to take and the steps included a time of rest for me with my family and our Father.

Again, GOD's divine orchestration is completely amazing.

Grateful!

Chapter 3   Significance of Albany, Georgia to America

Gaining an hour on the way to Nebraska was great.

Losing an hour while returning to Georgia ... not so great.

The best part of the journey: ***Our Father was talking to me the entire time.***

The trip was amazing with added blessings in the midst of dealing with auto issues (merely a slight concern), which led to divine appointments and introductions along the way. More confirmations of GOD's 'bigger plan' for these days.

The car was fully checked out before the trip. New tires and other key parts were added while in Nebraska. All should be fine. However, the oil light came on during a rain storm which came 'out of nowhere' within an hour, before I was in Iowa!

Checking on locations to have the oil checked while driving in rain and trying to watch for freeway exits during extensive road construction was a challenge. The first option was identified but, it was missed due to the road construction detour. Before I could find another location, the LORD confirmed I should wait until I am closer to Council Bluffs, Iowa.

This part of the journey would add another hour so I thanked GOD for keeping the oil concern in check and for finding a auto repair location close to a coffee shop!

Our GOD had a plan unfolding and before I found out how special it was, I was in a major conversation with Him about the location I preferred. This is funny now, because I personally want to think I am easy on GOD.

All of my words centered around one question since I did not want to go into Omaha from the 29 Freeway: *How can I get around in Council Bluffs when I've never been there before?*

Looking back on the 'event', I realize GOD was smiling the entire time I was chatting about silly stuff, for example: *'if something else is wrong with this car'* and other, related topics!

When I arrived at the Firestone Auto Care location, GOD prompted me to walk beyond the first desk and talk to the man at the next desk. The man had on a unique pair of safety glasses and he looked very official. I offered to provide my Firestone record to confirm I was not asking for a 'favor' when he stopped me and asked why I was there. When I said the oil light came on, he merely offered to go with me to my car now instead of requiring time for me to wait for an appointment. ***Favor from GOD!***

GOD wanted me to tell the man the car is my ministry car in Georgia. Before I could recheck with GOD to see why that would be important, the LORD was speaking through me and telling the man about the car being my ministry car in Georgia.

Before I realized what was happening, the man was responding! He said he is also in ministry in Council Bluffs.

In fact, he was not scheduled to work that day. He was called 'last minute' and he arrived at the shop just a few moments before I walked in the door. I was in awe while he tried to show me the evidence of the oil level being a bit low. In fact, I was still 'in awe' while I merely pointed to the back seat area of the car until I realized I needed to open the door and hand him the oil container I keep with me for just such a moment in time.

While he was adding the oil, he told me how the ministry was growing because they were blessing the people in the community as our Father asks us to do with each one, aka, love whosoever will come. Perfect confirmation of the return to Albany plan!

The oil was added. I walked back in the shop with him to check on the status of my Firestone account and find out how much I owe but, he said the details were not needed because he merely added oil which I provided.

Then, he asked me to wait a moment because he wanted to get something out of his vehicle.

When he returned, he handed me his ministry card and another card with a nice photo of a coffee cup.

Their message: *Loving GOD. Loving our neighbors.*

He was giving me a gift card for free cup of coffee from a specialty shop located within the Chamber office just a couple of blocks from Firestone.

GOD's favor, again!

Three blessings within moments due to GOD re-directing the plan from Nebraska to Council Bluffs, Iowa, a location I was visiting for the first time in my life!

1. Oil assistance 'for free' while meeting a deep man of GOD ministering in the region.

2. Cup of coffee I wanted to find, soon, 'for free'.

3. Another ministry testimony to share with Marty since Marty & Lynn are doing the same type of ministry in Albany.

As soon as I had my cup of specialty coffee 'in hand', I took a photo of the ministry card and sent it to Marty before I continued on my journey.

Albany, Georgia

It was immediately evident that Albany has taken some significant 'hits' within the body of believers.

A key pastor from the Brownsville Revival became the pastor of a local fellowship. Steps taken by him were fraudulent and they resulted in a Federal Prison sentence for him in 2014.

The large church and education buildings are located on a few acres. The size of the buildings would indicate the fellowship included a few hundred members. However, the status changed. The **For Sale** sign confirmed the presentation of the buildings would not immediately interest a buyer since they have clearly been vacant for several months.

LORD what has happened to the plans for Albany?

Marty and Lynn were prompted to commit to the community of believers. The LORD prompted them to build a small gathering location for a home fellowship. Then, as it grew, the LORD prompted them to build a chapel. GOD provided the exact location for Marty to place the stakes, markers which became the initial blueprint for building the chapel.

The chapel was built on their property. A fellowship gathered. It expanded. The people decided to lease a 'store front' location.

The fellowship ended. However, the chapel has remained as a gathering place for the region and it is available 7/24.

Marty and Lynn have remained as a strong pillar in the region while they have blessed many in the body of Christ through a program of helping Christians become debt free.

With 7/24 access and support, it seemed odd that the region was still 'stuck', still trying to figure out 'how to do revival'.

This is not a new status, region to region.

However, Brownsville Revival was clearly prophesied to move into South Georgia and specifically into Albany. LORD, what?

While I prayed, the LORD prompted me to return to be refreshed and restored within the bible study of Rebecca King.

It seems funny now but, in the same moment I was prompted to raise my hand and ask about a prophecy over Albany and the South Georgia region, a region Rebecca knows very well because she has lived in the region 'since birth', before I could insert a question or make a request Rebecca walked over to the white board to write the word Albany! She was prompted to review the same prophecy she had briefly shared with the bible study during 2014. Rebecca did not know I left Georgia or that I was in the Albany area!

Amazing moment since Albany was the exact point of the 'handle' of the prophecy with other towns identified within the pattern of the design of the prophetic word for the region:

Aladdin's Lamp Prophecy

Location: From Albany, South to Camilla and Thomasville; East to Valdosta and Northeast to Waycross; West to Albany through Tifton The flame started at Waycross, going Northeast to Jesup and the top stretched West to Hazelhurst and then South to Waycross.

Prophecy: Oil, fire starting in Sparks, Georgia; kindled in Alma with the word Alma defined as 'young virgin woman'. The use of the word was done to compare the move to be like the 'birth of Christ' through a young virgin woman, chosen by GOD to be the mother of HIS son. However, it is Alma in the Arabic language which is defined as a young woman. Other definitions: Alma means 'water'. Interesting to use Alma 'to kindle' the fire when water is used to put out a fire or stop a flame from becoming a fire.

The name Aladdin is Arabic and in Arabic it means: Adin of Alla or Servant of Alla / Allah. Adin also has a definition: 'sword of religion'. Therefore, the one who will take up the sword for the religion of Allah. Aladdin was used perhaps due to a definition where the word supposedly represented 'strong in the faith' or 'nobility of faith / nobility of religion'. However, the name is an Arabic name and represents the loyalty to the Muslim religion.

NOTE: *The LORD's pure religion is defined as feeding the lambs, especially seeing to the needs of the widows and orphans.*

All of this being said, the word was supposedly provided by the LORD. That presents a serious question. Why did the people not review the definition of the prophetic word, especially the names?

All of the churches in the region were notified.

Since 'revival' was the conversation, the churches trusted they would grow and the finances would flourish.

People attending the fellowships stated the growth plan resulted in pride and greed becoming evident and the impact upon the fellowship was negative.

That evening, I shared a copy of the map with Marty & Lynn!

The LORD confirmed the 'potential of revival' was stopped by the 'collision impact' of the Aladdin's Lamp prophecy. The prophecy became the focus without understanding or going to GOD for counsel, seeking GOD's wisdom about the meaning of the names or the steps to take. Instead, the churches trusted they needed to expand in size to take on the expenses for significant growth due to the 'flame of Aladdin's lamp'.

Growth took on a good amount of pride and greed. The actions taken stopped the move of GOD from expanding into South Georgia from the Brownsville Revival.

Exact location of the lamp covered the path from Brownsville (Pensacola, Florida) into and across the State of Georgia.

The people in the region confirmed they wanted revival and yet, nothing was taking place which resembled revival in their region. *LORD we repent for following man and leaning upon our own understanding! LORD forgive us!*

Revival lies & plan: It becomes a thought that 'a person brings revival' or when the move of GOD becomes evident 'having more church services' becomes revival. This is not aligned with GOD's plan. Often people trust the LORD sends me to bring revival to their region. Each of us are ambassadors of Christ, equipped to bring life more abundantly so the souls prosper! This is GOD's discipleship plan. We must be sure to align with His plans!

GOD was clear when He provided the vision after sending me on a journey *In Search of Wigglesworth.* **Bottom line:** If Christ resides in our hearts we would not 'flat-line' and require the blue cart for revival! GOD restores us! More prayer was required!

LORD I need a word and I need it now!

Our Father sent prophets with a word, even to small home fellowships.

In fact, I prayed with intensity for a word from someone who did not know me while I was driving nearly three hours from Albany to attend a home fellowship.

During the drive, I clicked and You Tube graciously repeated the special David Phelps song, *End of the*

Beginning while I cried out in song and in a loud voice for a word.

GOD heard my prayer.

A prophet was praying 'with intensity' while he was driving to the same home fellowship. The LORD prompted him to notice a specific person when he arrived: *A woman wearing glasses*.

The word became a perfect confirmation.

The prophet shared the word shortly after he arrived. The LORD actually told him the person would be wearing glasses and GOD would point them out as soon as he arrived.
The LORD arranged for the only open seat to be directly across from me, the woman wearing reading glasses. Within moments, he pointed to the hostess to start the recorder as he stood up and began delivering the word.

Thank GOD the blessings of a confirming word restore!

Then, the LORD took over and we went into the gift of laughter. The front of the room was immediately filled with the glory of the LORD! Prophet Chris Pittman invited all in the fellowship to join with us in the front of the room. Only a few walked forward and entered in with us.

The pattern of the prophetic words and the few who will 'enter in' has become a clear message regarding the status of the body of believers across America in these days! Sad, very sad.

Our Father has a great sense of humor and He wants us to join in with Him and be blessed with the gift of laughter for it truly becomes a gift of healing.

Restoration: GOD reveals what we need to know to 'be restored'.

GOD restores lives. When we repent, restoration takes place.

GOD restores relationships. Repent with each other or for each other and restoration will take place.

If you are not witnessing restoration it is time to 'check the heart' and be sure we are totally sold out to Christ and the will of GOD.

Hearing your thoughts, as Christ heard the thoughts of the people and answered before they asked, ***The answer is yes, GOD provides free will.***

GOD does not 'control everything' as people often state.

GOD is in charge but, our choices control our path in life. The choice to operate in GOD's will or our own free will is ours.

GOD's will, GOD's Kingdom plan. Free will, our plan!

Praying you will choose GOD's will, hear His voice and be restored!

GOD restores us, He restores regions and if we will continue to repent our LORD GOD will restore America because He restores nations. Repent with fellow believers, prayer warriors in the region and across America often and restoration will take place!

It's always been about restoration.

LORD reveal to us: What can we do to restore our lives, our relationships, our regions, states, and our nation, our America?

When the LORD reveals what we need to repent for, please take a moment 'in that moment' and REPENT!

LORD we are grateful Your hand is upon us!

There is so much we did not know, so much we did not bring to You to gain Your wisdom before we took action upon a prophetic word or the leading of humans. Forgive us LORD and help us forgive us for it is our desire to operate aligned with Your will, to do what we see and know You do and say what we hear You say and what You confirm in Your word.

Thank You for revealing so much truth to share during my 30 days in Albany and for loving us so much that You sent Your only SON! Help us remain so close to You we can hear You even when You whisper! We are eternally grateful for Your truth being revealed while we are here to do Your will on planet Earth!

AMEN. OUR GOD IS A FAITHFUL KING!

Chapter 4   Significance of Moultrie, Georgia to America

A funny thing happened while I was sharing the details during a night of honoring the funding sources for Millennial Kingdom Ministries. A special couple said they had to have my book right away. The books were 'on order'. They would arrive in a few days but, due to their urgent need they insisted they would buy the one I carry with me within the 'set of books' (12 of 17 released so far).

Long after they departed, they surprised the remaining guests who were still visiting and asking questions by returning to the meeting. They wanted wanted me to talk to their neighbor.

Three attempts to call the neighbor resulted in leaving messages. They were surprised. They always reached him when they called. A few days later they connected us. I made arrangements to stop by the home of the neighbor for a brief visit.

HISTORY: While living in Macon, Georgia and hearing a lot of 'unity talk' but, not seeing any results, he spent significant time with the LORD in prayer. During the process, he was prompted to move his entire family to Albany to help the people 'live in unity'.

Results: GOD sent him to Albany at the same time the other people were prompted by the LORD to move to Albany. However, they did not meet at any time during the 25 years, prior to my 30 days in Albany! The man spent his time meeting with the political decision makers in the region. He gathered nice proclamations, resolutions about unity for the two cities, Macon and Albany. Good ideas. A lot of unity talk. Some infrequent meetings with residents. However, unity was not evident. Nothing changed in either region.

GOD's Plan:

During his 25 years in Albany journey, he met a woman.

GOD told him that I was supposed to meet the woman.

My first phone call with the woman confirmed it would be good for us to meet in person.

The only thing I knew in that moment, our Father was clearly 'up to something'. How did I know this? There is a momentum, a quickening when the LORD's plan unfolds within hours and the days start to seem like a few hours!

Yes. The phone call(s) were extending into a few hours.

Yes. The one to two hour meeting at her home extended into a few hours.

Yes. The meeting was so powerful, I can honestly say *I experienced the 'deep presence of GOD' when we gathered together.* What I mean is GOD did it ALL for me this time.

When I speak, He often prompts me to be very clear and confirm the message is from Him and I am merely the messenger! It goes something like this, *It does not matter if you remember my name or not. What does matter is you remember our Father sent a woman your way and from this day forward your life will never be the same.*

On this day, our Father was doing it ALL for me!

On this first and only day in Moultrie during my lifetime, I met a woman named Denise Wilson-El 'in person' and since that day my life has not been the same.

Journeying into the deeper truth:

The first, second and third time Denise shared the facts, details which were 'new news' to me. I was clearly 'in a deep fog'.

During each of these times of hearing the deeper truth, I thought I was 'having a Southern moment' because *I have never heard such!*

It appeared she knew it was 'all new to me' because she graciously repeated the key facts a few times so I could begin to take it in and pray about the details.

Dr. Sandra Kennedy has shared a famous Kenneth Hagin quote which goes something like this, *It can take 50 times of listening to a sermon before the message is heard.*

These facts, the one Denise knew so well, are about our American history and they are 'far deeper' than a sermon! GOD was confirming it was urgent for me to hear the message so, I knew I only had the option to remain deep with the LORD when the deep truth was being shared each time.

The Holy Spirit will bring it all back to my remembrance when I remain deep with the LORD and make the request. It has helped me through many (make that multiple, many) situations!.

It felt like she was sharing the facts from different angles a few times but, I captured the depth of the truth after about five times. The moment I trusted I was grasping the facts, I started asking GOD for confirming words about this truth. Wow! He complied with my request immediately and in great detail!

A few facts already aligned with the specifics Nancy Cheek shared about the Native Americans being 'enslaved, placed on ships going up and down the coast at night, with some being dropped off in different regions and re-sold'. Children were taken from their parents. Spouses were separated and sold.

Marty spoke about the history in Albany with barges going up and down the river conducting auctions and hangings of Native

Americans sold as slaves. The depth of the truth shook me to my core. Denise repeated the same facts about her lineage, linked to Jesus Christ, with the ancestors being treated exactly the same way. They knew a few were brought from Africa but, only a few.

Immediately, the LORD confirmed 'author of confusion' which caused tears because the atrocities were carried out while listening to the enemy!

Trusting you are beginning to see how the truth of their lineage became a series of fragmented statements most of which were 'created' or 'fabricated', aka lies. Then, the lies were repeated so many times generation to generation, they started to seem like truth. Then, people started sharing the lies with their children 'as they heard the lies' and this is what has caused us to accept, live with and repeat the lies from generation to generation as though the lies were the truth. ***LORD we repent! Forgive us, LORD!***

At this point, I know it is a great time to take in a deep new breath of LIFE from our LORD because this deeper truth is foreign because it is so deep. The truth seemed harder to take in than lies!

LORD forgive us, we want life on earth to be like it is in heaven and we had no idea a deeper truth existed, a deeper truth which would help us know what to repent for and how to stand firm in truth to be able to set ALL of the captives free!

Denise was sharing the same facts about her family after she shared the deeper truth about her lineage with me, ***We are home.***

We did not come from anywhere. Yes, a few people were brought from Africa and inserted into the slave trade with people of color (red, black, brown, yellow and white) *and some were from other nations but, we are home. We have been here for centuries. This land was given to us by GOD. This land is our home.*

Denise is not from an Indian tribe. Denise may appear to be from Africa per the lies shared but, she is not from a lineage originating within the African slave trade. Denise is from a family who knows their roots!

She knows America is her home and her family lineage has been here for centuries. She has the proof 'in hand' which confirms her lineage is directly linked to the tribes of Israel and to Christ.

Wow! More deep, deep prayer required!

Powerful moments shared, especially when Denise shared how this family member 'beget' the next one and so on through her lineage back to Jesus Christ. I thought she was walking out of the bible for a moment in time to share this truth with me and then she would walk back in and continue on her journey. I was 'in awe'.

Holy Spirit tears fell over my bottom eyelids while GOD confirmed He was revealing the deeper truth to me within these moments of time spent Denise.

This is it! This is the very reason why I was not to include anything about what I thought I knew regarding roots of slavery & segregation in America within *For The Sake Of America.* Within six months after the book was released, GOD has revealed it to me!

Denise defined the 'status in this nation' before Europeans arrived and began changing everything about GOD's plan.

Denise confirmed <u>America had a different name</u>.

America was a nation operating in peace under **Divine Law.**

America (the new name given to this land) included everything the people needed.

America was **the promised land** the LORD provided for them.

When they arrived, the land was abundant, flourishing with enough for all to share. It remained this way for many, many centuries ... until about 1800. The 'what happened as of early 1800's' is revealed within *For The Sake Of America.*

It was clear to the people GOD sent to this land that ALL that was **already here, prepared for them by GOD and it ALL belonged to GOD.** They did not 'put their names on it' or 'sell it'. They lived in harmony and peace on the land GOD provided!

The pain of the separation of family members, the enslavement on the land which was freely given and freely shared with all who came during many, many centuries, changed when the Europeans saw the opportunity to sell the land for profit and charge taxes after deeds were established and people started claiming they owned what belonged to GOD, all that was provided by GOD for free for all to share 'while living on Earth'!

This was such a deep shock but, everything Denise shared resonated with me so deep while she spoke the truth and it was all taken to GOD in prayer. Everything!

More prayer required!

Personal phase of this journey. It was getting deep while I was witnessing and experiencing the 'stuck in the rut' status, also.

While returning from another journey to a special mechanic to find out why I was also 'unable to use the air conditioner' since arriving in Albany, I made my 'concerns' known to our Father.

In that moment a large white truck was in the lane next to my car while I was on Freeway 75 from Atlanta. GOD prompted me to take a picture of the white 18-wheeler in the next lane. It was just a plain, white truck! I did not get the point.

After a bit of 'Sheila logic' was shared, I agreed to take the picture. Later, I viewed the photo and I was surprised that some letters appeared on the back of the truck. I cropped the photo to see the words written in RED much easier:

We've Come This Far By Faith

More repentance prayers immediately required!

The LORD was being so specific, I was not laughing when I said *Georgia on GOD's Mind* was a chapter heading in *For The Sake Of America* so it would not be good as a book title.

Since I did not have a good title, I trusted I was not going to be writing an entire book about the deeper truth of the roots which were seeded in Georgia. However, the very next day while I was visiting Blackville Church of GOD with the same couple sitting behind me who prompted me to write the first book *For The Sake Of America,* our Father showed me a simple vision while I prayed.

The vision was only the cover of the book with the simple title: *For The Sake Of America II*. GOD kept it simple and I knew in that moment GOD was very serious about the facts being developed into a second book about the Significance of Georgia to America!

Chapter 5   Significance of Augusta, Georgia to America

Ah, Augusta!

My month in Albany was complete. The hosting option with Marty & Lynn would not be available again for 60 days.

They offered for me to return in 60 days however, I do not 'hang out'. Therefore, I was seeking our Father for the next step in the plan He has laid out before me in Georgia.

Within 24 hours, GOD confirmed *'there's a lot more to this story'.*

The seventh interview on Channel 49 in Augusta on my book *For The Sake Of America* was scheduled on June 22. I trusted 'after the interview' it would be time to pack and prepare to go somewhere in Georgia.

However, GOD prompted Dorothy (founder and host of Club 36 on Channel 49) to arrange for me to remain in Augusta that evening and GOD immediately provided confirmations.

Dorothy trusted I needed to attend the evening service with Dr. Sandra Kennedy because the same Barbara Houseman whom I met after the first TV interview in August flew in from Israel that day and she was going to be in Augusta through the weekend. I took it all to the LORD in prayer while Dorothy also needed some help at the studio for a few days and she trusted if a hosting home was available with someone attending the evening service, I would remain in the Augusta area for a while.

Barbara Houseman was speaking that evening and again on Sunday morning, Sunday evening and Monday evening. Powerful messages!

After the Thursday service, I asked a couple of people if they knew anyone who would be able to host me for a few days.

Deborah Hosey was prompted by GOD to have me 'come to her home for a while' late June 2017. This message from GOD is identical to the message the LORD gave to Denita Turner exactly one year before, late June 2016.

Friday, I returned to Macon. I packed the car and drove back to Augusta, to Whole Life Ministries for the Sunday morning service. It was a deep message so I spent private time between the morning and evening services with the LORD.

During the evening service, Barbara Houseman revealed the fact the lost tribes disbursed globally. Plus, she shared the list of

Kings over Israel and the fact 132 BC was the date the reign ended with the last King of Israel. Some of these details are listed within *The Ancient Book of Enoch* by Ken Johnson. Then, Barbara listed the elected terms of the Prime Ministers of since 1948 when Israel was recognized as a nation. The number of reigns and terms as of 2017 totals 58.

Barbara also shared that our 45th President's term aligns because the number of inaugurations in America as of the January 20, 2017 inauguration of President Trump is 58.

An additional unique historical fact about President Trump is that he was inaugurated when he was 70 years, 7 months and 7 days old in the year 5777 on the Hebrew calendar.

As soon as I followed my new host and hostess to their home that night and entered the room they prepared for me, I was in prayer about the facts Barbara shared.

Therefore, I barely unpacked any items from the car let alone arranged anything in an orderly manner. My heart and mind were so full, I merely went into deep prayer about the depth of the details shared and then I entered into deep rest in Him <u>after</u> GOD told me to look up the meaning of 58 in Hebrew.

Wow. Depth found in each definition of the meaning:
1. Withstand, having the ability to stand,
2. A temporary immunity or exemption; a reprieve,

3. Divine love and protection bestowed upon people,

4. An excellence or power granted by GOD,

5. State of being protected, sanctified by the favor of GOD,

6. Mercy, disposition to be generous; goodwill

And now, my favorite one of all. Drum roll please ...

7. I insure you that I assure you that I am the only true living LORD

In Complete Awe

Amazing night. Facts shared which align with what the LORD has revealed. Then, the LORD prompted me to re-focus my prayers upon the depth of truth shared by Denise during our moments in Moultrie.

LORD reveal Your truth about the land. If this land was the promised land and we were to be united and operate under Divine Law. If You sent Your tribes to this land centuries before it was renamed America, please confirm with a sign so I know that I know the truth revealed is Your truth and people 'on the land' have become aware of Your truth.

This was my prayer focus the entire time with our Father. A prayer which concluded at our regular time, by midnight, when I finally left it all with the LORD and entered into rest with Him.

About 8:20 the next morning, my first morning at my new hosting home, I heard a knock on my bedroom door with an invitation to go to Healing Springs if I could be in the car by 8:30.

Yes was my answer while I had no idea where my clothes were or how I would be able find what I would need to throw myself together within 10 minutes.

Hosts were new to me. They did not know about any of the details in **For The Sake Of America** or what the LORD was showing me after arranging for my to return to Georgia. They had no idea what I was praying about the night before. They did not even know I am an author! GOD has a great sense of humor!

Healing Springs

The first sign I saw at Healing Springs:

GOD's Acre; Land Deeded Back to GOD
No Option for a Transfer of Title

Six British Soldiers, During the Revolutionary War

Left for Dead with the Native Americans, to be Buried

In Six Months, they Returned to their Regiment

Fully Healed and Healthy

GOD'S ACRE
HEALING SPRINGS

ACCORDING TO TRADITION, THE INDIANS REVERENCED THE WATER FOR ITS HEALING PROPERTIES AS A GIFT FROM THE GREAT SPIRIT. THEY LED THE BRITISH WOUNDED TO THEIR SECRET WATERS DURING THE AMERICAN REVOLUTION AND THE WOUNDED WERE HEALED. THIS HISTORICAL PROPERTY HAS BEEN DEEDED TO GOD FOR PUBLIC USE. PLEASE REVERE GOD BY KEEPING IT CLEAN.

If you visit the Springs be sure to take some water bottles and fill them with the amazing water.

Then, do yourself a big favor. Take off your shoes and put your feet in the water.

The water was analyzed and it contains numerous minerals including:

Barium,

Calcium,

Cadmium,

Magnesium,

Manganese,

Sodium,

Phosphorus,

Silicon,

Zinc.

As you enter the area of the actual spring, beyond the pipes which provide a consistent, steady flow, you will notice a cross.

The sign reads:

Open Your Hearts.

Behold I stand at the door, and knock; if any man hear my voice, and open the door, I will come in to him, and dine with him, and he with me. **Revelation 3:20.**

LORD thank You for being with us, the same yesterday, today and tomorrow, while we WAKE UP! Thank you for standing with us while we repent and turn from our wicked ways, so our lives, our families, our regions and our land known as America will be healed, restored.

A special commentary was shared by James (Jimmy) Murray during my seventh interview regarding *For The Sake Of America* on Channel 49, Club 36, in North Augusta:

Feds forced 17,000 from homes, marched to Oklahoma!

Gold had been discovered in Georgia in 1828, resulting in a Democrat-controlled Congress rushing through the Indian Removal Act, which passed by a single vote in 1830. It was signed by Democrat President Andrew Jackson and carried out by Democrat President Martin Van Buren.

Over 12,000 Cherokees signed a petition in protest of the Indian Removal Act. Condemning the Federal Government's mandate were members of the National Republican Party and the Whig Party, including: Rep. Abraham Lincoln, Senator Henry Clay, Senator Daniel Webster and Congressmen Davy Crockett.

The Cherokee were largely Christian and even had their own language and alphabet, created in 1821 by Cherokee silversmith Sequoyah.

Christian missionaries led resistance to the Federal Government's removal of the Indians, with many missionaries being arrested by the State of Georgia and sentenced to years of hard labor. Some were arrested for their opposition to Indian removal and their case went to the U.S. Supreme Court.

Chief Justice John Marshall ruled in favor of the Cherokee in Worcester v. Georgia (1832), writing that *the Cherokee Nation was a "distinct community" with self-government "in which the laws of Georgia can have no force."*

He (also) said, *"Thanks be to GOD, the Court can wash their hands clean of the iniquity of oppressing the Indians and disregarding their rights."*

Noting that the Supreme Court had no power to enforce its edicts, but had to rely on the President to actually implement them, Democrat President Jackson was attributed with saying: *"John Marshall has made his decision; now let him enforce it!"*

James Murray credits the information as research provided through an organization established by Bill Federer and chronicled through his web site: www.americanminute.com

The Native Americans knew the truth.

They knew about the land.

They knew about the springs.

They knew it all came from GOD. *They shared the truth!*

Since I am not easy on GOD, I prayed, asking for a second example of the people 'in current generations who knew the truth'.

Within a few days, a friend insisted we had to stop on our way to a meeting. Since I wanted to arrive early, I denied the request. After the meeting, the LORD insisted I stop by the location where the smallest church was built.

As soon as I saw the entrance sign, I realized why GOD insisted!

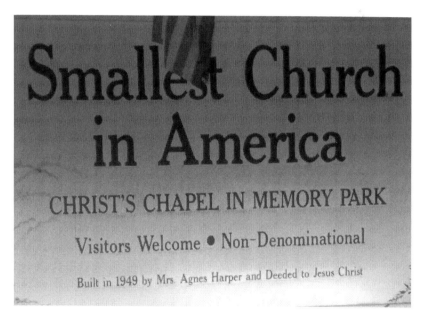

Smallest Church in America, Deeded to Jesus Christ

OK.

I get it.

GOD is confirming the deeper truth.

 More prayer required!

Chapter 6   Significance of Ancient Roots in America

There are deep roots which affect America to this day.

When we repent for the 'top layer' and nothing changes, we need to dig for the next layer by seeking the LORD and requesting that He reveal the next layer. Repentance is a process!

Too often, repentance is only used for the 'surface facts'. ***LORD help us repent for each layer, all the way back to the root!***

Again, the first time I heard the details about a deeper truth which revealed we have not known the identity of the Native Americans, people enslaved on the land they were freely given by GOD, I was in complete shock. Then, the LORD sent confirming words from various sources and two of His sources shared reference materials which confirmed the deeper truth is the truth!

The first time I heard about people 'being home' and declaring to me that GOD sent them to this promised land centuries ago and it was a peaceful nation for centuries while they operated under divine law, I have to admit I was a skeptic!

The second time our Father sent me to the Healing Springs with my hosts, our friend Heather wanted to go along with us.

She was late. While we were waiting, the LORD insisted a copy of *For The Sake Of America* needed to be in the car. I did resist a bit since the Springs are a place of sand, water and mud. Therefore, it made sense to me that it is not a great place for me to be carrying a book. Trusting GOD was smiling when I put the book in the car.

Our lunch time was extended due to divine appointments so, we arrived about 30 minutes after we would have left the Springs.

Within three to five minutes, GOD prompted me to turn and view a rental car entering the parking area. GOD told me to talk to the driver about the Springs.

The man was interested in seeing the signs and the information about the six British soldiers. Then, he said that GOD was prompting him to tell me, *This land is his home. His ancestors did not come from Africa ...* wow.

In fact, the LORD sent him to Augusta this weekend to meet the man who has all of the documentation to prove what he was telling me. He was only at the Springs due to the man with the facts being told by GOD to leave his residence in Atlanta and stay in a specific hotel in Augusta, Georgia.

Due to this move, several people have flown to Augusta to meet with the man. My new friend would not have been at the Springs if his flight was to Atlanta vs. Augusta. He shared the same amazing facts which were revealed during their time together as Denise shared during our time together. Then, the man visiting the Springs for the first time was instructed to go directly to the Springs before flying back to Maryland.

The man was not at the Springs more than five minutes. He sings in the choir at his church on Sunday mornings so he had to quickly return to Augusta for his flight to Maryland.

While he was preparing to depart, the LORD prompted me to hand him a copy of my *For The Sake Of America* book which I resisted bringing to the Springs. ***LORD, I repent! Forgive me!***

More moments of standing in awe. GOD orchestrated each of the delays within the planned schedule to go to the Spring so I could meet a man from Maryland who would confirm the exact same facts Denise shared with me during our phone calls and our brief visit at her home one afternoon in Moultrie, Georgia. GOD sent the man with all of the documentation from Atlanta to Augusta so the schedule world work out in His timing for the divine appointment!

In the same week, I returned to the Rebecca King bible study where we met in 2014.

On the way, I stopped to see my special Macon friend, Elizabeth. Before I could fully share the *'have you ever heard such'* details with Elizabeth, she walked over to her bookshelf and pulled out a specific book to hand to me, *He Walked The Americas* by L Taylor Hansen. Hansen was an archaeologist who studied to prove it was not possible. Instead, the facts were proven by the artifacts and the testimonies of the native people across America and beyond.

The native people saw the LORD descend from the heavens and walk across the ocean. They described Him as bright white while it did not mean he was 'white' as we describe skin color. He was appearing to them 'in the glory' as He did on the Mount of Transfiguration, formerly Mount Hermon. Did you know the Mount of Transfiguration was actually the ancient Mount Hermon?

This was 'new news' to me!

Mount Hermon was the highest mountain in the region; on the border of Israel & Syria. It was a focus area for Israel during the six-day war in 1967. The UN has positioned a permanent location known as the **"UN buffer zone"** on the top of Mount Hermon.

Enoch was aware Mount Hermon was the location where the oaths were sworn by the Watcher class of fallen angels to take wives among the daughters of men. Jesus changed history when He appeared, glorified, transfigured on this mountain!

Enoch was Noah's great-grandfather.

The Ancient Book of Enoch by Ken Johnson confirms Enoch knew deep truth direct from living in the days and from our Father.

He describes the ancient history of Mount Hermon and many facts we do not recognize easily since the book of Enoch is not included within the bible.

GOD prompted me to look up the direct lineage from Enoch to Noah.

Methuselah. Enoch's son and Noah's grandfather, Methuselah (means 'his death shall bring judgment'), lived 969 years. He died on the 11th of Cheshvan, seven days before the flood.

Lamech. Enoch's grandson and Noah's father, Lamech (means 'to make low') died at 777 years, five years before the flood.

Noah. Enoch's great-grandson Noah (means 'rest, comfort') died at 950 years, 350 years after the flood.

After the flood, the life span reduced significantly with Moses being 120 years old when he went with GOD. The people only knew 'Moses was no more', as Enoch & Elijah. Some translations of the bible state *GOD buried Moses.* People have looked for the bones of Moses for centuries without being able to provide a bone.

GOD re-focused the Journey to the Lost Tribes of Israel.

Repeatedly, our Father has drawn my attention back to facts about the lost tribes. They were the ten tribes in Northern Israel, tribes which were originally 'carried off' by the King of Assyria.

More new facts were provided within hours:

The lost tribes were given land, abundant with everything they needed and they were protected in their journey by our Father.

The facts about the disbursement of the tribes are clearly stated within the Second Book of Esdras in The Apocrypha.

The land the King of Assyria took them to 'as captives' was identified as the ancient land of Azaerath.

When Barbara Houseman shared the chart of the reign of Kings within Israel and the fact the reigns ended in 132 BC, I immediately put the two facts together and trusted the lost tribes traveled the year and a half to the new land in 132-134 BC.

I was wrong!

Once again, I started leaning on my own human understanding before allowing the LORD to continue to direct my research.

Another wow moment. ***LORD, I repent! Forgive me, LORD!***

The Book of Second Esdras confirms the name of the man given the responsibility of leading the people to the new land GOD provided. His name was Shalmaneser, King of Assyria.

In the ancient times, there were land masses within the current day oceans. Plus, the Atlantic ocean was not as large of a mass of water as we know it today. While researching the facts, I found details regarding an earthquake in 1755 which nearly doubled the size of the Atlantic ocean. Not focused upon geography, yet!

Regardless of how much water or what was required to make the journey, the people who knew the LORD was guiding them were eager to go, grateful to leave the heathen population In Israel to go to a land where the human race had never lived.

They went through the narrow passages of the Euphrates River and the LORD held back the sources of the river, all of the water, until they passed over and continued their journey of one and a half years. The country was called Azaerath.

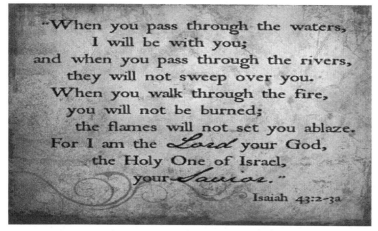

"When you pass through the waters,
I will be with you;
and when you pass through the rivers,
they will not sweep over you.
When you walk through the fire,
you will not be burned;
the flames will not set you ablaze.
For I am the Lord your God,
the Holy One of Israel,
your Savior."

Isaiah 43:2-3a

Personally, I took a few breaths after finding out these details.

Then, I quickly searched through the ancient map book to find the date the lost tribes were taken away by King Shalmaneser.

They did not go in 132 BC.

The journey did not show up until 721 BC!

Plus, The Apocrypha confirms the LORD promised to hold back the sources of the rivers, all of the water, for the tribes to pass through as they left and He will, again, upon their return to Israel.

However, the ancient map book states:

> *Never to return, hence called 'THE LOST TRIBES'.*
> *The end of the Kingdom of Israel.*

More prayer required!

Prophets were sent to me to confirm Christopher Columbus was not Christopher Columbus. At first, I had no idea what they were referring to because I was taught that Christopher Columbus was the famous sea captain who discovered America.

Nothing about the true identity of Columbus was shared in a history class!

His actual name was Cristobal Colon, a Jewish family with roots back to their Jewish lineage in Italy.

Spain expelled some Jews, imprisoned, convicted and burned some at the stake for refusing to eat pork and they forced many to convert by being baptized in the Catholic church.

Later, the ones who were forced to convert and be baptized were imprisoned, burned at the stake or expelled.

Regardless of how the Jews were removed from their homes and businesses, their wealth, ALL of their property and assets, were confiscated and sold with ALL of the cash going into the treasury of King Ferdinand (also of Jewish descent) and Queen Isabella.

For his efforts, King Ferdinand became known as His Most Catholic Majesty in 1492. In recent times, Queen Isabella was submitted by nomination to the Vatican for sainthood due to her worthwhile efforts in unifying Spain and spreading Christianity.

In 1974 the Catholic church actually granted Queen Isabella the prestigious title: *Servant of GOD.*

Cristobal / Christopher last name Colon / Columbus arranged to delay his departure one day after his armada of ships were packed and ready to depart. Many scholars indicate the delay was due to the fact Colon was honoring the day of mourning for the destruction of the first and second temples of Jerusalem. His delay seems to indicate he had knowledge of the Hebrew calendar and the fact that departing on that specific Jewish day of remembrance would result in not being blessed on the journey.

Regardless, the steps taken against the Jews in Spain are clear, Columbus benefited from their losses. Coincidence? The forced departure of the Jews was arranged on the same day the voyage of Columbus began. Did he collect from both sides of the conflict?

Scholars also believe Columbus used the facts disclosed within The Apocrypha to find the location of the land where the LORD directed the lost tribes of Israel, a land which supposedly became the newly named America by Columbus.

Whether Colon/Columbus used the facts to discover the new land of America or not, the man named Colon remained with his name identified in history books as Columbus for the remainder of his life. No matter where the funds came from, he chose to not disclose his true Jewish heritage or identity.

Personal phase of the journey.

Three weeks after being directed to Augusta, the ministry car was rear-ended.

Major prayer.

Extra time and effort required by my hostess in taking me to the grocery store and to run errands. Seemed like I was right back where I was in the early days in Georgia. Plus, the accident resulted in the insurance company of the responsible driver for the accident to total my car within a few days due to age and mileage.

Therefore, I went from having a reliable (albeit, a 1999) vehicle which was well maintained with new tires and other expensive parts added within the past few weeks, to not having a car.

In the midst of my 'upset', GOD simply directed my attention to the beautiful sunset as my hostess was driving back to the house. We were close to her home. The curves and trees were starting to cover the sunset while I raised my phone to take a picture. So, I told GOD, *I'm sorry I missed my chance.*

However, GOD simply said, *Take it now.*

One click and it was done. At first, I only knew it was a nice picture of the trees and the sun shining through.

I was about ready to put my phone away as we entered the driveway when the LORD said, *I AM here. I AM with you.*

GOD prompted me to check the picture on my phone again, to expand the photo and take a second look. Wow.

Tears!

The cross is clearly formed within the picture.

Repentance required, again!

Even in the little things, it is important to keep the slate clear!

My 'stuff' is so minor compared to what He is sharing with me and how He is guiding me through the depth of truth!

The glory shining through was amazing. It was enough.

Then, the fact a cross appeared within a large circle of His glory which is impossible 'in the natural' among the trees in the dark, wooded area.

He caused me to stand in complete awe of Him, again!

Chapter 7   Significance of Ancient History to America

It was Saturday morning:

While I continued to pray about all of the details shared during the week, a week which seemed like a year squeezed into a week, our Father was reminding me of the glorious plans He has for me, for each of us who love Him! Confirmed in **I Corinthians 2:9.**

While I was deep in prayer, our Father directed me to the book of Ezekiel.

When I reached to pick up my bible, He told that He wanted me to look up Ezekiel in the Chronological bible. As soon as I located the book of Ezekiel, I was supposed to wait until my hostess returned from a bible journaling class. What? That class was going to take up the entire Saturday morning.

Realizing patience is a virtue, I truly tried to be patient.

This step in the journey was absolutely intriguing.

Immediately, I was busy questioning GOD about what my hostess would have to do with me looking up a book in the bible?

GOD was completely silent!

In this moment, I did everything I could to NOT tap a pencil on the table while I waited minute upon minute upon minute!

A lot of minutes passed while I was waiting!

GOD chose to fill the moments with His deeper truth. He refocused me upon the chronological bible while He prompted me to remember a little bit about our early days together in Georgia.

In October 2013, when GOD sent me to Georgia for three weeks, I packed a suitcase. GOD added the lap top. The trip was planned as a 'time of rest' so I did not bring my study bibles or reference books.

After it was clear I would be 'in the area' a little while longer, GOD prompted me to arrange for a ride to the Christian bookstore since I was without a car during the first 18 months of this journey. He prompted me to buy a specific bible which He said was on sale.

This was in February of 2014.

The first book published during my days in Georgia, *It's A Faith Walk!* was released a few days before this special day.

Excited, I immediately made plans!

GOD knew the only bible on sale was the chronological bible and the only money I had available 'in my pocket' was just enough to buy it since it was the only bible included in the half price sale.

GOD was making it clear the 'cash on hand' was exactly what I needed while I had no idea what I was going to do with a chronological bible. It was not part of my reference bibles, ever.

GOD did not refer to this bible at any time since February 2014, until this very day.

While waiting, GOD gave me an amazing vision about my life. Within the vision, He confirmed exactly how He provided all things for me to live abundantly and prosper 'on earth'.

He reminded me that He provided and supplied everything for me when He sent me. He provided everything required, every day.

After He arranged my destination 'on earth' He still cared for all of my needs in my mother's womb. He kept everything within me and around me alive and at peace. He made sure all was well.

Then, when the plans changed during the moment of birth, everything changed. I entered into a world of bright lights, significant 'white noise' and to obtain anything from anyone in the world I had to learn how to speak their language and use my own free will.

He showed me how it has changed, generation to generation, since His truth was not passed on and the world based success plan became the focus. Yikes! That was an eye-opening moment!

Then, he revealed what I did to 'make a name for myself' without realizing it, competition arose as I gained degrees and acknowledgments from the world, pride and greed often took hold of my thoughts since I was not trained to hear His voice to be directed step by step. I was clueless. I had no idea life could be easier and better if our Father was allowed to direct my path.

So much was revealed which I had not repented for, specifics which were putting distance between me & the LORD.

He showed me the difference if I would have known the path my steps would take by aligning with the world, allowing my life plan to be taken over and fueled by pride and greed. Yikes, again!

To remain successful, compromises with the world took place.

The world influenced more and more of my decisions.

Compromises caused me to depart from GOD's plan for me.

It was amazing to see a vision of my life and how GOD's plan for me, the glorious plan He has 'in store' for each of us, became affected and at times totally infected with the dis-eases attached to the roots of the world based plans.

Lots of repentance prayers required!

Things became idols without realizing it was even happening.

Commitment to others and to organizations resulted in me choosing time with world 'stuff' and therefore committing adultery against my Father by not keeping my relationship with Him as my number one focus!

This was the deepest view of my life our LORD has revealed to me. It was a deep time of realizing that my life as a Christian was not quite as tight with the LORD as I had thought. Recent years are good while prior years were not so good and the depth of truth when GOD revealed roots requiring repentance from actions of prior generations were tough to see because He gave me a wagon load of truth which I also needed to repent for! ***LORD forgive me!***

Tough, yet I am deeply grateful!

When GOD did this, I knew there was a much deeper meaning and a much bigger reason for me to realize these facts in this hour.

GOD was revealing the deeper truth about me and my ancestors: ***Roots are deeper than we realize 'on the surface'.***

When I was living in good times, I took really good care of me and a friend or two in need while I was not aware of what others needed and I did not 'see to the widow or the orphan'.

When I hit the hard times straight on, I cried out to GOD to find out what He was going to do for me and how He could let all of this could happen to me since I am clearly His child, a joint heir.

Today, GOD was showing me I was NOT the first in my family to experience any of this, I was NOT the first to feel the depth of pain due to the specifics. I was merely 'another one' in the family!

Yikes. GOD was going deeper than He had ever gone before.

Some roots He revealed are a few years old and some are actually generations and centuries old. I knew this was possible going back generation to generation however, GOD was making it very clear to me in this moment how deep the roots are with my 'issues' and 'situations'! ***LORD, I repent! I will share Your truth with the generations and help the body of believers get back on track!***

It was a bit of a surprise to me, since we have pastors and missionaries in the family line while the roots of departing from

GOD's plan run deep in prior generations in both sides of the family, and in me! *LORD, forgive me!*

Tears were abundant.

GOD was filling every second with His wisdom as only He can while I was waiting for Deborah to return!

As soon as GOD completed the vision …

Deborah Returned

The moment Deborah entered the house, I began telling her the details GOD shared in the morning and how our GOD has a great 'treasure hunt' sense of humor by preparing me to hear deeper truth about me while I was waiting for her return!

Deborah was surprised and a bit concerned because she did not have a chronological bible but, while I was explaining how different this version of the bible is and how the chapters of the book are not in the same order in the many versions of the bible since the books in the bible are not in chronological order so they do not confirm how the centuries unfolded.

As I continued to show Deborah the order of the chapters since they are completely 'out of order' within the chronological bible, I noticed my explanation was becoming confusing. Before I went too far into the details, GOD stepped in and prompted Deborah to bring out her newly purchased ancient chronological map book.

Wow.

Even though the chronological bible confirms the books of the bible are 'not in order' and even the chapters within the books are 'not in order', the chronological bible and the chronological map are an exact match.

Deborah was smiling because she had no idea what she was going to do with the map until this moment! She merely liked how the map book looked so she bought it but, she did not know what to do with the map book once she owned it. When I showed her how the map lined up with the chronological bible, we both stood in awe staring at the map.

The centuries were defined top to bottom with the names of the nations, the kings ruling the nations, the insurgents at war with the nations, the prophets of the time, etc., etc., etc.

It was so fascinating! We were prompted to point out various details which we remembered from bible stories over the years.

Then, it was Sunday morning:

It was a special plan I committed to every time I go to a location, to enter into the meeting or the sanctuary one to two hours early.

This is something I prefer to do because it gives me time to enter in with the LORD and be ready for the deep messages our Father shares with me when believers unite together in fellowship.

Typically, what the LORD is revealing to me is separate, a message He is sharing with me vs. the 'topic of the day'.

When I pulled out my small travel bible, I asked which scripture I should focus upon. GOD kept it simple. He had one question, *We are still focused upon Ezekiel, right?*

Smiling as I nodded without realizing it and I opened my bible to Ezekiel. Then, I waited a moment before He revealed which chapter. After a few moments of enjoying the praise team rehearsal, GOD prompted me to turn to **Ezekiel 16.**

GOD's Love for Jerusalem

Again the word of the LORD came to me, saying, [2] *"Son of man, cause Jerusalem to know her abominations,* [3] and say, 'Thus says the LORD GOD to Jerusalem: *"Your birth and your nativity are from the land of Canaan; your father was an* A*morite and your mother a Hittite* [4] *As for your nativity, on the day you were born your navel cord was not cut, nor were you washed in water to cleanse you; you were not rubbed with salt nor wrapped in swaddling cloths.* [5] *No eye pitied you, to do any of these things for you, to have compassion on you; but you were thrown out into the open field, when you yourself were loathed on the day you were born.*

[6] *"And when I passed by you and saw you struggling in your own blood, I said to you in your blood, 'Live!' Yes, I said to you in your blood, 'Live!'* [7] *I made you thrive like a plant in the field; and you grew, matured, and became very beautiful. Your breasts were formed, your hair grew, but you were naked and bare.*

⁸ *"When I passed by you again and looked upon you, indeed your time was the time of love; so I spread My wing over you and covered your nakedness. Yes, I swore an oath to you and entered into a covenant with you, and you became Mine," says the LORD GOD.*

⁹ *"Then I washed you in water; yes, I thoroughly washed off your blood, and I anointed you with oil.* ¹⁰ *I clothed you in embroidered cloth and gave you sandals of badger skin; I clothed you with fine linen and covered you with silk.* ¹¹ *I adorned you with ornaments, put bracelets on your wrists, and a chain on your neck.* ¹² *And I put a jewel in your nose, earrings in your ears, and a beautiful crown on your head.* ¹³ *Thus you were adorned with gold and silver, and your clothing was of fine linen, silk, and embroidered cloth. You ate pastry of fine flour, honey, and oil. You were exceedingly beautiful, and succeeded to royalty.* ¹⁴ *Your fame went out among the nations because of your beauty, for it was perfect through My splendor which I had bestowed on you,"* says the LORD GOD.

Jerusalem's Harlotry

¹⁵*"But you trusted in your own beauty, played the harlot because of your fame, and poured out your harlotry on everyone passing by who would have it.* ¹⁶ *You took some of your garments and adorned multicolored high places for yourself, and played*

the harlot on them. Such things should not happen, nor be. ¹⁷
*You have also taken your beautiful jewelry from My gold and My
silver, which I had given you, and made for yourself male images
and played the harlot with them.* ¹⁸ *You took your embroidered
garments and covered them, and you set My oil and My incense
before them.* ¹⁹ *Also My food which I gave you—the pastry of
fine flour, oil, and honey which I fed you—you set it before them
as sweet incense; and so it was," says the LORD GOD.*

²⁰ *"Moreover you took your sons and your daughters, whom
you bore to Me, and these you sacrificed to them to be devoured.
Were your acts of harlotry a small matter,* ²¹ *that you have slain
My children and offered them up to them by causing them to
pass through the fire?* ²² *And in all your abominations and acts
of harlotry you did not remember the days of your youth, when
you were naked and bare, struggling in your blood.*

²³ *Then it was so, after all your wickedness—'Woe, woe to
you!' says the LORD GOD—* ²⁴ *that you also built for yourself a
shrine, and made a high place for yourself in every street.* ²⁵ *You
built your high places at the head of every road, and made your
beauty to be abhorred. You offered yourself to everyone who
passed by, and multiplied your acts of harlotry.* ²⁶ *You also
committed harlotry with the Egyptians, your very fleshly
neighbors, and increased your acts of harlotry to provoke Me to
anger.*

27 *"Behold, therefore, I stretched out My hand against you, diminished your allotment, and gave you up to the will of those who hate you, the daughters of the Philistines, who were ashamed of your lewd behavior.* 28 *You also played the harlot with the Assyrians, because you were insatiable; indeed you played the harlot with them and still were not satisfied.* 29 *Moreover you multiplied your acts of harlotry as far as the land of the trader, Chaldea; and even then you were not satisfied.*

30 *"How degenerate is your heart!"* says the LORD GOD, *"seeing you do all these things, the deeds of a brazen harlot.*

Jerusalem's Adultery

31 *"You erected your shrine at the head of every road, and built your high place in every street. Yet you were not like a harlot, because you scorned payment.* 32 *You are an adulterous wife, who takes strangers instead of her husband.* 33 *Men make payment to all harlots, but you made your payments to all your lovers, and hired them to come to you from all around for your harlotry.* 34 *You are the opposite of other women in your harlotry, because no one solicited you to be a harlot. In that you gave payment but no payment was given you, therefore you are the opposite."*

Jerusalem's Lovers Will Abuse Her

³⁵ 'Now then, O harlot, hear the word of the LORD! ³⁶ Thus says the LORD GOD: "Because your filthiness was poured out and your nakedness uncovered in your harlotry with your lovers, and with all your abominable idols, and because of the blood of your children which you gave to them, ³⁷ surely, therefore, I will gather all your lovers with whom you took pleasure, all those you loved, and all those you hated; I will gather them from all around against you and will uncover your nakedness to them, that they may see all your nakedness. ³⁸ And I will judge you as women who break wedlock or shed blood are judged; I will bring blood upon you in fury and jealousy. ³⁹ I will also give you into their hand, and they shall throw down your shrines and break down your high places. They shall also strip you of your clothes, take your beautiful jewelry, and leave you naked and bare.

⁴⁰ "They shall also bring up an assembly against you, and they shall stone you with stones and thrust you through with their swords. ⁴¹ They shall burn your houses with fire, and execute judgments on you in the sight of many women; and I will make you cease playing the harlot, and you shall no longer hire lovers. ⁴² So I will lay to rest My fury toward you, and My jealousy shall depart from you. I will be quiet, and be angry no more. ⁴³ Because you did not remember the days of your youth, but agitated Me with all these things, surely I will also recompense your deeds on your own head," says the LORD

GOD. *"And you shall not commit lewdness in addition to all your abominations.*

More Wicked than Samaria and Sodom

[44] *"Indeed everyone who quotes proverbs will use this proverb against you: 'Like mother, like daughter!'* [45] *You are your mother's daughter, loathing husband and children; and you are the sister of your sisters, who loathed their husbands and children; your mother was a Hittite and your father an Amorite.*

[46] *"Your elder sister is Samaria, who dwells with her daughters to the north of you; and your younger sister, who dwells to the south of you, is Sodom and her daughters.* [47] *You did not walk in their ways nor act according to their abominations; but, as if that were too little, you became more corrupt than they in all your ways.*

[48] *"As I live,"* says the LORD GOD, *"neither your sister Sodom nor her daughters have done as you and your daughters have done.* [49] *Look, this was the iniquity of your sister Sodom: She and her daughter had pride, fullness of food, and abundance of idleness; neither did she strengthen the hand of the poor and needy.* [50] *And they were haughty and committed abomination before Me; therefore I took them away as I saw fit.*

[51] *"Samaria did not commit half of your sins; but you have multiplied your abominations more than they, and have justified*

your sisters by all the abominations which you have done. ⁵² *You who judged your sisters, bear your own shame also, because the sins which you committed were more abominable than theirs; they are more righteous than you. Yes, be disgraced also, and bear your own shame, because you justified your sisters.*

⁵³ *"When I bring back their captives, the captives of Sodom and her daughters, and the captives of Samaria and her daughters, then I will also bring back the captives of your captivity among them,* ⁵⁴ *that you may bear your own shame and be disgraced by all that you did when you comforted them.* ⁵⁵ *When your sisters, Sodom and her daughters, return to their former state, and Samaria and her daughters return to their former state, then you and your daughters will return to your former state.* ⁵⁶ *For your sister Sodom was not a byword in your mouth in the days of your pride,* ⁵⁷ *before your wickedness was uncovered. It was like the time of the reproach of the daughters of Syria and all those around her, and of the daughters of the Philistines, who despise you everywhere.* ⁵⁸ *You have paid for your lewdness and your abominations,"* says the LORD. ⁵⁹ For thus says the LORD GOD: *"I will deal with you as you have done, who despised the oath by breaking the covenant.*

An Everlasting Covenant

⁶⁰ *"Nevertheless I will remember My covenant with you in the days of your youth, and I will establish an everlasting covenant with you.* ⁶¹ *Then you will remember your ways and be ashamed, when you receive your older and your younger sisters; for I will give them to you for daughters, but not because of My covenant with you.* ⁶² *And I will establish My covenant with you. Then you shall know that I am the LORD,* ⁶³ *that you may remember and be ashamed, and never open your mouth anymore because of your shame, when I provide you an atonement for all you have done,"* says the LORD GOD.

Tears. This is what has happened to America!

GOD revealed, we are in this exact place in America!

Will we repent?

Will we re-align with Him?

Will GOD re-establish His covenant with us?

For years, I asked top leaders in the body of Christ to help the believers realize America has become a Sodom and Gomorrah.

They did not agree. Everything 'looked good' to them.

To stop the conversation, they actually told me that the end times cannot be changed so if things are getting really bad then it means we are 'in the end times'.

LORD I thank you for keeping Your hand upon us, caring about us, doing everything you can to wake us up as a body of believers so we will become the remnant as you describe us within The Apocrypha.

Then, it was Monday afternoon:

Physical therapy appointment with Aaron Cohrs, also a member of Dr. Sandra Kennedy's Whole Life Ministries.

My first statement to him regarding GOD directing me to research Ezekiel on Saturday caused Aaron to excuse himself for a moment to find a specific scripture within his bible.

Aaron was so excited because GOD was prompting him to immediately share a specific scripture before I revealed any facts.

As soon as Aaron opened his bible to Ezekiel 16, I was 'in awe'.

GOD told Aaron to go to this chapter of the bible, read it and then make a note about it: *America, revealed by GOD on March 2, 2011.*

For a moment, I was speechless.

It might have been a very short moment in time for Aaron but, I was clearly speechless.

March 2nd of 2011 in the year of our LORD was a critical point in time, a pivot point in my life. The LORD revealed to me, again, the depth of injustices I have experienced are 'minor' compared to the atrocities experienced by the people who are called by His name in America.

On the same second day of March in 2011, nearly seven years before I met Aaron, GOD was revealing the same depth of the status of America to Aaron. Our GOD placed the facts so deep in Aaron's heart that he has prayed about these details *For The Sake Of America* since that day.

II Chronicles 7:14. *If My people who are called by My name will humble themselves, and pray and seek My face, and turn from their wicked ways* (REPENT), *then I will hear from heaven, and will forgive their sin and heal their land* (RESTORE).

Significance of Ezekiel's word to Jerusalem & America:

The captivity and enslavement of the 'lost tribes' and the Native Americans, realized all people are formed in the image of GOD and yet appearing 'on earth' with various outer skin colors. However, ALL on earth have the same blood in their veins.

II Chronicles 7:14. *If My people who are called by My name will humble themselves, and pray and seek My face, and turn from their wicked ways* (REPENT), *then I will hear from heaven, and will forgive their sin and heal their land* (RESTORE).

Ezekiel was a Prophet when the tribes of Israel were disbursed.

Promised land was provided to the tribes of Israel by GOD.

Native Americans for many centuries, lived peacefully.

The lost tribes from Israel 'in America', lived in peace.

Divine Law was followed by all who lived on the land.

Living in peace, freely sharing all the LORD provided.

No title documents or deeds established for human ownership.
Everything we have done to change from GOD's plan requires repentance. Then, the LORD can restore us and the land.

Within *For The Sake Of America,* I included a brief note about a prophecy GOD revealed to Prophet Stephen Powell. Briefly, *The wealth of America as of 1885 will be restored if the people in America will repent and proceed as outlined within:*

II Chronicles 7:14. *If My people who are called by My name will humble themselves, and pray and seek My face, and turn from their wicked ways* **(REPENT),** *then I will hear from heaven, and will forgive their sin and heal their land* **(RESTORE).**

Whatever we did not realize in the current generation each time we were merely repeating lies about the people and how we were told they believed and lived, REPENT and seek FORGIVENESS so we can be RESTORED as individuals, as regions and as the nation of America.

The Native people in America knew the Holy One, the Spirit of the Heavens, the Father of the Sky and the Ocean, the Spirit of the Water (witnessed when He was seen walking from the horizon line toward the people as a brighter and brighter white image while crossing the ocean to be with them). Many of the elders across America and beyond saw Christ and His disciples. The accounts of the healings are amazing. He was described as knowing more than 1000 languages, resolving conflict, uniting the people the moment he entered their region and all diseases were healed!

Those who were enslaved (being of many shades of color from light to dark) during many centuries BC to many centuries AD have called upon Him and cried out to Him in song while working in the fields, trusting He heard their cries.

When the nation of America was established as a separate country, the formation was established based upon the words provided within the Divine Law upon which the Native Americans lived.

They did not want to create 'enmity' between them and the LORD so they endured and stood firm, for in their hearts they knew the truth. The LORD helped them while they endured so much due to atrocities committed against them by people operating outside of GOD's will and GOD's counsel.

LORD there is so much you are revealing in these days. Grateful you are revealing to us what we have done in our generation and what our ancestors have done in the prior generations. Thank you for bringing to our memory the steps taken in our free will which were not aligned with Your will. Help us to see what needs to be done so Your will is what is done 'on earth' so it will become on earth as it is in heaven. Forgive us LORD for everything done in ignorance or if we have had some or full knowledge of our actions and what they would do to affect the lives of others and cause them to depart from you for the time to repent is today! Help us to know what we have done and what can be done to restore what has destroyed lives in family, extended family and in our America.

Chapter 8   Significance of The Remnant

So much conversation 'in these days' about being part of the remnant or not.

Personally, I pray I will stand firm as Stephen stood when he was being stoned. Praying I will have the strength in that hour to 'be in the moment' with the LORD and still be true to His word as confirmed by Stephen after He preached the truth to the devout, the loyal ones up until the moment they stoned him to death.

Acts 7:54-60 (emphasis added).

When they heard these things <u>they were cut to the heart</u>, and <u>they gnashed at him with *their* teeth</u>. 55 But he, <u>being full of the Holy Spirit</u>, <u>gazed into heaven</u> and <u>saw the glory of God</u>, and <u>Jesus standing at the right hand of God</u>, 56 and said,

"Look! I see the heavens opened and the Son of Man standing at the right hand of God!"

57Then they cried out with a loud voice, stopped their ears, and ran at him with one accord (NOT in unity, 'in one accord' in God's truth); **58** and they cast *him* out of the city and stoned *him*. And the witnesses laid down their clothes at the feet of a young man named Saul. **59** And they stoned Stephen as he was calling on *God* and saying, *"Lord Jesus, receive my spirit."* **60** Then he knelt down and cried out with a loud voice, *"Lord, do not charge them with this sin."* And when he had said this, he fell asleep.

Would we be willing to seek forgiveness for all involved?

If Stephen neglected to ask that the people be forgiven, would Saul have been in a position 'in his life' to become Paul 'in a moment' during his ride to Damascus to continue how he operated in life as Saul of Tarsus?

Repentance is for us and for **each life** we impact with our words and our actions. It's a two-way process. Repenting for what we have done or what others have done. Clearing both directions.

Who is the remnant? One example:

Romans 11:4b.

Response from the LORD. *"I have reserved for Myself seven thousand men who have not bowed the knee to Baal."*

The first few times I heard a prophet tell me that I am here for the seven thousand who have not knelt, I had no idea what the LORD wanted me to do. Back then, I did not know about Baal, either.

Looking back, my questioning the LORD about the plan resulted in being sent forth to nearly every continent and given the opportunity to see the truth about our life as supernatural representatives of the LORD through GOD's eyes during the process. Life has not been the same since the LORD showed me what He sees in us.

A pastor who operated in the gift of prophecy shared the word about my life plan being linked to the 7,000 who have not knelt and he also shared that he saw the LORD taking me up Jacob's ladder and when I would go up a step, I would go back two.

This seemed a bit confusing in that moment.

However, the LORD did proceed in my 'training program' and He showed me stepping out in faith and then, leaning upon Him or taking a step or two back with Him for a bit, before going forward again.

Immediately after I returned from Europe, I received an urgent call from him with the request to preach for him the next Sunday because GOD told him I would have a word for the people.

My moments were filled with prayers crying out to GOD to know that I know the word I would have for the people.

Facts: The pastor and his wife were given an all-expense paid trip to Hawaii for their 35th wedding anniversary.

Status: Associate pastor announced to the congregation that the LORD was going to bless the 50 families who are to go with him to form a separate fellowship from the senior pastor.

Intense prayers about all of this while I waited to hear the word from the LORD for the people.

When I arrived, I was grateful the pastor was extremely busy with the praise team.

Why? The word the pastor was sure the LORD had revealed to me for the people was not revealed to me, yet.

The moment before the microphone was handed to me, the LORD thanked me for being empty. He was so right!

Then, He assured me that He would fill me with the words when they were needed.

The microphone was handed to me. No words, yet.

Prayers were still 'in process' because the words were needed now. GOD wanted me to enjoy viewing the congregation, connecting with the people while the words were 'on the way'. Prayers with our Father, prayers of thanks and in tongues in the moments of viewing the people in the fellowship. Then, the LORD revealed through me that *it is critical for the people of GOD to know His voice and to realize there are only two kingdoms operating 'on earth', GOD's Kingdom and Baal, and this helps us distinguish which voice is speaking to us at any given time.*

Then, the LORD prompted me to use my other hand to cover the backside of the microphone and share words as they were shared by the associate pastor, *While the senior pastor is away, the LORD wants fifty families to leave with me and establish a new fellowship...*

The affect of covering the back of the microphone with my hand made the request sound more like the enemy than the moments when the associate pastor merely smiled, stood upright and delivered the sentence as though it was merely a sentence for the people to pray about before making their decision.

When people are not able to discern, it becomes easy to follow words of deceit because the delivery is so subtle!

When the truth 'is not in them' as the scriptures confirm, the ability to make a choice which aligns with the will of GOD is nearly impossible.

The senior pastor was not able to 'let it go'. The hurt he felt from this status remained in his heart and mind for the remainder of his days, days which were few due to an illness which took over his body shortly after this 'incident'. He did not regain his health.

LORD we repent for what we hold on to which brings disease to us! Show us ALL of the facts LORD so we can repent! Forgive us LORD! LORD we repent! Forgive us, LORD!

When GOD's people hear His voice, they obey!
We have a choice: We obey or we disobey.
Delayed obedience is disobedience. Disobedience is sin.
Thank the LORD we can repent. Then, obey!

Grateful our Father makes it simple for us, while the 'doing of it' is not as simple because we are human and we 'hold on' to stuff!

Atrocities have been committed against GOD's people 'on the land' and they have gone on for many, many centuries. Repent!

Asking GOD to forgive in a blanket prayer is not sufficient.

We are to 'know the truth' and 'operate in the truth'.

Now that we know the deeper truth:

Confirm salvation and the fact we are grafted into the body!

Become 'born again' as ONE NEW MAN.

Highly recommend: *One New Man Bible*

Subtitle: *Revealing Jewish Roots and Power*

Why? The Hebrew language is a LOVE language.

The most important commandment is to LOVE.

Go to GOD with everything!

Remind ourselves: We are no longer Gentiles.

Seek His counsel.

Obey GOD's commands.

DO NOT BECOME RELIGIOUS!

REMEMBER:

The devout, the religious ones killed Christ & the disciples.

The devout, the religious ones killed the men around Martin Luther, the men around Tyndale, and then Tyndale because they brought the truth to the people.

Israel's Rejection Not Final. Romans 11:16 For if the firstfruit *is* holy, the lump *is* also *holy;* and if the root *is* holy, so *are* the branches. **17** And if some of the branches were broken off, and you, being a wild olive tree, were grafted in among them, and with them became a partaker of the root and fatness of the olive tree, **18** do not boast against the branches. But if you do boast, *remember that* you do not support the root, but **the root *supports* you.**

How Native Americans Were Treated. The Atrocities: Stone Inscription, Dated 500 BC; Evidence Found to Prove the Cherokee who Preserved the Hebrew Language (Paleo Hebrew from 500 BC)

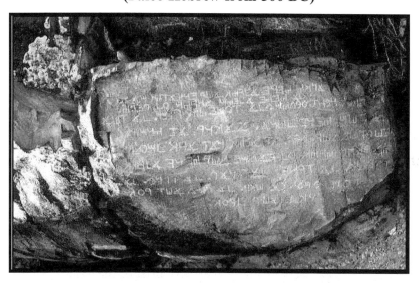

Ten Commandments Found in New Mexico

Combined Cherokee & Hebrew dictionaries exist

Research & Repentance is an On-going with all Sources

Do not limit Native Americans to the title 'Indians'

Actions, ancient and those carried into current day through current generations, were and are ungodly.

The treatment of the Native people, the Native Americans who lived on the land freely and in peace requires repentance.

The truth must become a part of the repentance prayer in our lives, our families, our regions, spreading region to region, state to state across our America.

Then, we are NOT to return to 'how we operated and thought' before the truth was known to us!

The atrocities were extensive in Georgia. Slave ships up and down the coast and on the rivers, including auctions and hangings!

After a recent interview at Channel 49 in Augusta, an audience guest looked across the table and told me: *My ancestors were Cherokee. We know we are part of the lost tribes of Israel.*

Do not limit Native Americans to a skin color!

Do not make decisions based upon skin color!

ALL colors are represented in the people.

ALL are made in GOD's image!

Significant repentance and forgiveness required!

LORD we repent!

LORD forgive us for we did not know the truth! Right here and now, LORD. We stand in truth with You! Keep Your hand upon us! We know repentance of the lies when the truth is revealed will restore us! Help our families unite & restore; help people repent in the regions and states across America so Americans will unite together & America will be restored!

GOD your promise is what we are standing on in this hour! You declared an angelic vortex was positioned over Macon, Georgia and Moravian Falls, North Carolina, unto Your prophets For The Sake Of America. We come to you in full repentance for when we repent and forgive ALL in Georgia, South and North Carolina, Your blessings will flow across the region and then, spread across America 'like a mighty flood'! We thank You & praise You for the flow & the flood, LORD!

In **The Ancient Book of Enoch,** so much truth is revealed.

Enoch was the great-grandfather of Noah.

Enoch is another servant of GOD who was taken direct to heaven by the LORD with the statement appearing in **Genesis 5:24.** *And Enoch walked with GOD; and he was not, for GOD took him.* Also in **Hebrews 11:5.** *By faith Enoch was taken away so that he did not see death, "and was not found, because GOD had taken him"; for before he was taken he had this testimony, that he pleased GOD.*

Enoch describes **The Ungodly within End Times Outline.**

The Ancient Book of Enoch

Outline 5:4-6. The ungodly.

But you do not patiently endure trials, nor obey the commandments of the LORD; instead, you have turned away and spoken great and swelling words with your impure mouths against His majesty.

You hard-heated ones will find no peace. Your days will be shortened and your lives cursed! You will die and spend eternity in hell; you will not obtain *the Mercy.*

In those days you will give up your peace, and not only the righteous, but the sinners and ungodly, will curse you.

Outline 5:7-9. The Godly.

Salvation (Yeshiva) will be for the elect, but not for the sinners. But the elect will inherit the earth with light, joy, and peace. Then wisdom will be given to the elect and they will live eternally and never sin again through ungodliness and pride. They will be humble and prudent. They will not die in the time of wrath when their number is complete; but instead, live in peace with the number of their years multiplied eternally.

The Apocrypha includes facts we have not known since it was removed from our bibles. It was included within the 1611 King James bible but, it was removed in in the mid-1800's. The Apocrypha also describes the remnant:

The Second Book of Esdras, 13:21+ (emphasis added)
Explanation of vision given to Ezra.
Verse 29+. Behold, the days are coming when the Most High is going to deliver those who are on the earth, and amazement will come upon those who live on the earth, and they will plan to make

war one upon another, city upon city and place upon place, people upon people, and kingdom upon kingdom.

32 And it will come about, when this happens that the signs will occur which I showed you before, and my Son will be revealed, whom you saw as a man coming up.

33 And it will come about, when all the nations hear his voice, that every man will leave his country and the wars that they have with one another, and a countless multitude such as you saw will be gathered together, wishing to come and subdue him. But he will stand on the top of Mount Zion. And Zion will come and be revealed to all men, made ready and built like the mountain that you saw carved out without hands.

37 And my Son will charge the heathen who have come with their ungodliness (this was symbolized by the storm), and will upbraid them to their face with their evil thoughts and the tortures with which they are to be tortured (which were symbolized by the flame), and he will destroy them without effort by the Law (which is symbolized by the fire).

39 And as for seeing him gather about himself another multitude that was peaceable, **these are the ten tribes that in the days of King Hoshea were carried away from their own land into captivity, whom Shalmaneser, king of Assyria, made captives, and carried beyond the river; they were carried off to another country. But they formed this plan among themselves, to leave the heathen population, and go to a more distant region, where the human race had never lived, so that there**

perhaps they might keep their statutes, which they had not kept in their own country. And <u>they went in by the narrow passages</u> of the Euphrates River. For the Most High then did wonders for them, for he held back the sources of the river until they had passed over. But it was a long journey of a year and a half to that country, and the country is called Azaerath.

46 There they have lived until the last time, and now, when they are about to come again, the Most High will hold back the sources of the river again, so that they can cross over, It is on that account that you saw the multitude gathered together in peace. But those also who are left of your people, who are found within my holy borders, will live. Therefore it will be that when he destroys the multitude of the nations that are gathered together, he will protect the people that remain, and then he will show them many, many wonders.

IF only the tribes of Israel and those grafted into the body of believers shall be the remnant, will we proceed with repentance to know that we know we will be part of the remnant?

Repentance for how ALL were treated for centuries, ancient to current, will clear our record and the record for our America.

Restoration will become evident AFTER we have repented for breaking up their families, for stealing the land from them to 'sell for profit' when they knew it all belonged to the only true living

LORD. There is so much to repent for as we realize the message of our LORD to Jerusalem is His warning to us in America!

The warnings are not new!

The acts of man which are against GOD's will are not new!

The people we admire in the bible were not perfect!

Moses killed a man.

King David had a man killed & married the man's wife.

Miriam was a gossiper.

Thomas was a doubter.

Martha was a constant, consistent worrier.

Elijah was depressed, often.

Paul, as Saul, ordered the killing of many believers.

When we say we stand for the truth, we must be willing to be the ones who speak truth! There is hope for us! The ultimate calling forth, Lazarus. He was dead! Are we willing to give our ALL and not judge others when we are forced to choose? It was the devout, the loyal, the religious who judged GOD's elect:

Christ was crucified.

Peter was arrested, crucified upside-down.

Philip was crucified.

Barnabas was stoned to death.

Matthias (took the place of Judas), beheaded in Jerusalem.

James, brother of John, beheaded in Jerusalem.

James, brother of Jesus, after preaching in Jerusalem; thrown off the roof of the temple (100 feet) and yet, he continued to praise the LORD so he was beaten to death with clubs.

Jude was killed by arrows.

Andrew was crucified while preaching the gospel.

Thomas was killed by a pagan priest's spear while in India.

Paul was arrested, taken to Rome, tortured, taken to the chopping block and beheaded. In that very moment, he was saying: *I have fought a good fight, finished my course. I have kept the faith. I have run my race. Henceforth there is laid up for me a crown of righteousness and not for me only but for all those that love his appearing.* He put his head on the block & legend says he was speaking in tongues when the ax fell.

Matthew was killed by sword in Ethiopia.

Mark was dragged behind horses in Egypt until dead.

Luke was arrested in Greece by Roman Empire & hanged.

John survived everything done to kill him. He had more work to do. He wrote the last book.

Revelation 1:5-6 *And from Jesus Christ, who is the faithful witness, and the first begotten of the dead, and the prince of the kings of the earth. Unto him that loved us, and washed us from our sins in his own blood, And hath made us kings and priests unto GOD and his Father; to him be glory and dominion for ever and ever. Amen.*

Thank you James Murray for helping me with the facts for some of the names on the list of the patriarchs and martyrs!

LORD we repent and ask You to forgive us!

Chapter 9   Significance of America in 1880 and 1980

Brief Summary, Inserted from *For The Sake Of America*
Faith Monument

The Faith Monument is a granite monument <u>dedicated in 1889,</u> located within a residential community above Plymouth Rock.

Faith Monument stands 81 feet tall and weighs several ton.

Faith is at the top of the monument. She points to Heaven, to our Creator. She is holding an open bible, the basis of our faith

Paid by Congress; Dedicated 1889

Faith monument includes four separate sections which display images confirming exactly how we can proceed to retain our liberty and freedom:

1. Morality is holding the Ten Commandments in her left hand and the scroll of revelation in her right hand. At the base of the throne are the engravings: **Evangelist** and **Prophecy.** She has no eyes. She looks inward because liberty must be in us before it will show up within the nation.

2. Law founded upon the bible, the source of truth as the Pilgrims **General Laws** confirm: *...by how much they (the laws) are derived from, and agreeable to the ancient Platform of GOD's Law."* The two carved items under the throne where **Law** is seated represent **Justice** and **Mercy.**

3. Education is holding an open book of knowledge, the Bible. Her throne has two carvings: **Youth** receiving instruction and **Wisdom** represented by a grandfather who points to the bible while standing a globe, confirming both parents and grandparents are to teach the youth from a Biblical perspective. She is wearing a **Victory** wreath for focusing the youth upon the truth and the way to proceed in their life, resulting in the *training up a child in the way he shall go so when he is old he will not depart from it* as confirmed within **Proverbs 22:6.**

4. Liberty is seated with a sword in his hand. He is prepared to protect the family and liberty. Two carvings: **Tyranny** and **Peace.** The images clearly confirm why the Pilgrims / Puritans were known as the ***Parents of America, the Republic*** confirmed by the the Founding Fathers.

New Facts:

Within the Ancient Book of Enoch, the accounting of the fallen angels is described in great detail. Well worth the read to realize their flesh was destroyed but, their spirits are 'here' until the day of Judgment! There are only two kingdoms to choose from: 1 GOD's Kingdom, the LORD's Plan, 2 World based Kingdom, Satan's Plan.

Which Kingdom will you choose to align with each day? I love the quote: **Be the kind of person that when your feet hit the floor in the morning Satan says, *Oh NO!* (Insert your name) *is up!*** Will you become one more believer who will operate in truth, share the truth far & wide and insert your name to become a force the enemy has to reckon with every single day? I hope so! Praying with you!

Brief Summary Georgia Guidestones in Elberton, Georgia

Inserted from *For The Sake Of America*

○

Nearly 100 years after Faith Monument, unveiled in 1980

Four Guidestones in eight specific languages: English, Spanish, Swahili, Hindi, Hebrew, Arabic, Chinese, and Russian.

Paid with private funds, anonymous; a check from R. C. Christian.

About 4 AM, the LORD was directing me to research the new, global monetary / currency structure: BRIC.

BRIC was formed in 2008. South Africa insisted they are to be part of the structure; added in 2010. Structure changed to BRICS.

The languages are an exact match to BRICS!

1. **Brazil** (Spanish and English),

2. **Russia** (Russian and English),

3. **India** (Hindi and English), and

4. **China** (Chinese and English).

5. **South Africa** (Swahili and English) recently insisted the country was supposed to be included and this resulted in the the name change from **BRIC** to **BRICS**.

BRICS established as BRIC in 2008 is the acronym for an association of five major emerging national economies: Brazil, Russia, India, China, and South Africa. Originally the first four were grouped as 'BRIC', before the controversial addition of South Africa in 2010.

The Guidestones are located just East of the Hartwell Highway on Guidestones Road out in the country about nine miles north of the center of Elberton, Georgia.

The granite slabs are 19 feet, 3 inches, positioned at the highest point in Elbert County, about 90 miles east of Atlanta, Georgia.

Ten messages align directly to pagan/Baal focus upon nature:

1. Maintain humanity under 500,000,000 in perpetual balance with nature.

2. Guide reproduction wisely – improving fitness and diversity.

3. Unite humanity with a living new language.

4. Rule passion – faith – tradition – and all things with tempered reason.

5. Protect people and nations with fair laws and just courts.

6. Let all nations rule internally resolving external disputes in a world court.

7. Avoid petty laws and useless officials.

8. Balance personal rights with social duties.

9. Prize truth – beauty – love – seeking harmony with the infinite.

10. Be not a cancer on the earth – Leave room for nature – Leave room for nature.

If you have an opportunity to visit the Guidestones I trust the LORD will prompt you to observe but, **do not touch**.

The world-based plan is not filled with blessings for GOD's people. The world-based plan established the Georgia Guidestones in 1980, nearly 100 years after the Faith Monument was dedicated.

New Facts:

R C Christian was not the name of the man obtaining the account or providing the check. The granite company in Elberton tried to discourage the man who submitted the request by increasing the bill beyond comprehension. The man did not try to negotiate. He informed the granite company employees a group of loyal Americans worked on this project for 20 years.

Separate group of people, loyal to their cause, vandalized the stones. They painted slogans. A few examples: 1. *Death to the New World Order.* 2. *You will not succeed.* 3. *Jesus will beat you (u) Satanists.* The FBI was called in to help with the situation.

In January 2015 when we visited the stones, Sheriff's deputies were 'at the site' within minutes of our cars entering the 'out in the country, within a cow pasture' location to observe the people until they left the site. A video camera in the center was evident.

In June of 2016 when we visited the stones, a full video surveillance system was evidently installed to protect the stones from a remote location.

America was a blessed nation 'under GOD' and we had every opportunity to live in freedom and liberty by receiving the truth through the Native Americans, then, the Pilgrims. Everything was at peace. Since those days we have operated exactly as the oppressors of ancient times, ancient kingdoms, ancient structure of the Pharisees by becoming judges of others and not loving those made in Your image!

We have become a people which are not easy to recognize in the world because we have become too much like the world for the non-believers to see a difference!

We have not sought the truth from You, from the bible, so we have become so worldly the competition to become successful in the world is showing up everywhere, in everything, in every area of our lives, between siblings and between spouses, between children and parents and it has allowed the access of evil motives to enter into the hearts of even those who profess to know You and serve you.

LORD, forgive us and help us while we open our hearts and minds anew to Your deeper truth being revealed, to allow Christ to reside deep in our hearts and renew the resurrection power in us, and allow our minds to be conformed to the mind of Christ!

LORD reveal ALL to us in these days so we can fully serve you and share the truth to the four corners of the earth!

II Chronicles 7:14. *If My people who are called by My name will humble themselves, and pray and seek My face, and turn from their wicked ways* (REPENT), *then I will hear from heaven, and will forgive their sin and heal their land* (RESTORE).

When was Ezekiel a prophet? From 930 to 586 BC.

When were the tribes disbursed from Israel? 721 BC.
LORD we repent for the tribes of Israel being placed in captivity in Assyria as of 721 BC.

LORD we thank you for preparing a 'new land' where humans had never resided so the tribes would have a new land to occupy and continue to honor you and follow your statutes.

When was Babylon established & maintained? 559-330 BC.
LORD we repent for the days while Babylon was being formed and for allowing it to continue for 229 years.

When did Nehemiah re-build the wall around Jerusalem?
The re-build began in about 445-444 BC.
LORD we thank you for prompting Nehemiah to give up his position in the court of the King to return to Jerusalem and rebuild the wall.

Jerusalem Wall:
Some returned to assist with the re-build of the wall.

Some living along the length of wall did not participate.

Some repaired their portion of the wall.

Some who lived along the wall did re-build their section.

The enemy threatened to destroy the wall again when they heard Nehemiah gathered the people together and the wall was being re-built.

Nehemiah gathered the people together, again, and assured them of the promise of the LORD if they would re-build so they aligned together with the LORD GOD and continued to work on the wall until it was completed.

Interesting to realize what it was like for Nehemiah to go door to door and make the request and receive either a positive, negative or middle of the road response. The responses given do not appear to be ancient!

The exact facts are provided within the book of Nehemiah.

Esther became Queen.

In this same time frame, Esther became Queen.

She brought truth to the King to make the right decision!

On the next Sunday:

Trusting the book was complete, it seemed odd the LORD prompted me to carry the travel bible with me.

As soon as I entered the sanctuary, however, the LORD prompted me to read about the prophet Joel.

At the beginning of the book, the definition of the name Joel or Yo'el is provided. *Joel means Yahweh is GOD.*

It also confirmed the fact Joel was a prophet during the reign of King Joash (835-796 BC), the same time of Ezekiel.

GOD directed my attention to **Joel, Chapter 1:13-20.** In that moment, I was prompted to remember a partial page from the bible which survived the devastating fires in Pigeon Forge and Gatlinburg which began in November 2016.

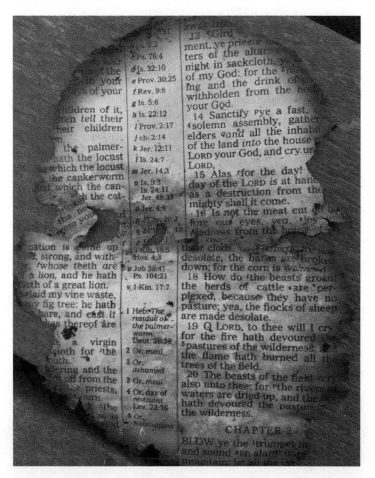

Joel 1:13-20, Page of the Bible at Dollywood After Fire

An employee of the Dollywood Theme Park in Pigeon Forge, Tennessee found the partial page of the bible near a bench during the clean-up days at the park and he shared it on social media.

The year since the fires in Pigeon Forge and Gatlinburg have been filled with devastating events, significant earthquakes, volcanic eruptions even in locations where glacier ice was still evident, historic hurricanes and much more.

This is why the reading of **Joel 1:13-20** was so significant.

Mourning for the Land

13 Gird yourselves and lament, you priests;
   Wail, you who minister before the altar;
   Come, lie all night in sackcloth,
   You who minister to my GOD;
   For the grain offering and the drink offering
   Are withheld from the house of your GOD.

14 Consecrate a fast,
   Call a sacred assembly;
   Gather the elders
   And all the inhabitants of the land
   Into the house of the LORD your GOD,
   And cry out to the LORD.

15 Alas for the day!
   For the day of the LORD *is* at hand;
   It shall come as destruction from the Almighty.

16 Is not the food cut off before our eyes,
   Joy and gladness from the house of our GOD?

17 The seed shrivels under the clods,
　Storehouses are in shambles;

　Barns are broken down,
　For the grain has withered.

18 How the animals groan!
　The herds of cattle are restless,
　Because they have no pasture;
　Even the flocks of sheep suffer punishment.

19 O LORD, to You I cry out;
　For fire has devoured the open pastures,
　And a flame has burned all the trees of the field.

20 The beasts of the field also cry out to You,
　For the water brooks are dried up,
　And fire has devoured the open pastures.

Surely, this is a true wake-up call to the remnant!

Then, the LORD said, *There is more.*

Our Father immediately prompted me to turn to Nahum.

I must admit, I did not know much about Nahum. The LORD had not drawn my attention to him before.

In this moment, our Father wanted me to review the paragraphs before the beginning of Nahum, Chapter 1.

It begins with a scripture:

Luke 12:48. *For everyone to whom much is given, from him much will be required.*

Then, the paragraph describes the assignment for Nahum:

The Hebrew word Nahum ('comfort', 'consolation') is a shortened form of Nehemiah, Comfort of Yahweh.

Nineveh was given the privilege of knowing the one true GOD. Under Jonah's preaching this great Gentile city had repented, and GOD had graciously stayed His judgment. Wow.

GOD focused on Jonah a lot in our 'early journeys' together. He sent so many people to remind me of the three days of Jonah in the whale story. I thought I was being obedient in a 'do diligence' sort of way by seeking someone 'more qualified' to go on the assignment. My 'delayed obedience' was actually disobedience. GOD revealed it to me very gently when I finally agreed to go and yet, in the same moment I added a 'left jab' comment: *It is hard to believe all of the other people told you no!* GOD gently whispered, *Every time you delayed the assignment* (for about three and a half years) *you were telling me no.* OUCH!!!

After all of the training since 'those days' here I was, again, with GOD realizing I was going to bypass the Jonah information because 'we have been there and done that' was my thought. GOD urgently prompted me to remain focused and read on: *however, a hundred years later, Nahum proclaims the downfall of this city. The Assyrians have forgotten their revival and have returned to their habits of violence, idolatry, and arrogance. As a result, Babylon will so destroy the city that no trace of it will remain – a prophecy fulfilled in painful detail.*

LORD forgive us! We have become like Nineveh!

GOD gave us the structure to build the foundation.

GOD gave us the laws, His commandments.

GOD told us exactly what to do to live in liberty & freedom!

GOD provided the land and all that was needed, in abundance.

What did we do?

We departed from GOD's plan.

We made a different plan.

What were we thinking?

We kept adjusting the plan and aligned with the 'system'.

What were we thinking?

We went silent! In fact, we became the 'silent majority'.

What were we thinking?

GOD sent major revival to America 100 years ago. Here we are, today, 100 years later, after Azusa Street, after the revivals early in the 1900's in England, having returned to significant habits of violence, idolatry and arrogance!

LORD forgive us! The Ten Commandments were preserved 'in Hebrew' for centuries and now, we cannot keep the Ten Commandments within the court houses in our new nation!

We are at choice! We are to possess until He comes!

What were we thinking?

GOD sent Jonah to Nineveh and the 120,000 were saved.

100 years later, Nahum went to Nineveh and witnessed their truth, they returned to their habits of violence, idolatry and arrogance!

II Chronicles 7:14. *if My people who are called by My name will humble themselves, and pray and seek My face, and turn from their wicked ways (REPENT), then I will hear from heaven, and will forgive their sin and heal their land (RESTORE).*

Will Jesus recognize us as 'My people' or will He say He never knew us?

Chapter 10   Americans Are At Choice

Choose Liberty & Freedom, *For The Sake Of America!*

May the truth shared within these pages bless you, fill you to overflowing, and cause you to share it with all members of your family, extended family, all friends, fellow believers, and those who seek the truth and want a relationship with the only living LORD, the Father, the Son and the Holy Spirit.

May all in your household, family and extended family, be able to declare: as for me and my house, we will serve the LORD!

LORD we are grateful that You have given us Your truth in Your Word. We are thankful You reveal it to us, for we do know You sent Your Son to us 'in the world' as the Savior, Prince of Peace, the Word, the Way, the Truth and the Light.

Proverbs 22:6.

Train up a child in the way he should go,
And when he is old he will not depart from it.

Steps We Can Take, Today!

1. Gain a close relationship with the LORD, today!

    Seek His truth!

    Align with His will! Speak His truth!

    Knowing He never leaves or forsakes us.

    Knowing we are more than conquerors.

    Knowing we are the head and not the tail.

    Knowing who we represent when we walk in faith.

2. Humble ourselves.

3. Pray.

4. Seek the LORD in all things.

5. Repent of free will and align with the LORD's will.

6. Turn from our wicked ways.

7. Wait upon the LORD. Repent and align with His will!

8. Listen for His voice; receive confirmation from Him.

9. Unite together with members of the body of Christ.

   Share the truth with whosoever will come to hear truth!

   Pray repentance prayers with each one; restoring life.

10. He will honor our prayers.

11. He will forgive our sins.

12. He will heal us, our land, each community & nation!

II Chronicles 7:14. *if My people who are called by My name will humble themselves, and pray and seek My face, and turn from their wicked ways (REPENT), then I will hear from heaven, and will forgive their sin and heal their land (RESTORE).*

Resurrection Power. Romans 8:10-11.

And if Christ is in you, the body is dead because of sin, but the Spirit is life because of righteousness.

But if the Spirit of Him who raised Jesus from the dead dwells in you, He who raised Christ from the dead will also give life to your mortal bodies through His Spirit who dwells in you.

Christ <u>resides</u> in us! We have <u>resurrection power</u>!

We are responsible!

We cannot blame the Government, Congress or the Media!

Within the Declaration of Independence, **We The People** have the opportunity and the responsibility to counter the actions of the government.

We hold these truths to be self-evident, that all men are created equal, that they are endowed by their Creator with certain unalienable Rights, that among these are Life, Liberty and the pursuit of Happiness.--That <u>to secure these rights, Governments are instituted among Men, deriving their just powers from the consent of the governed, --That whenever any Form of Government becomes destructive of these ends, it is the Right of the People to alter or to abolish it, and to institute new Government, laying its foundation on such principles and organizing its powers in such form, as to them shall seem most likely to effect their Safety and Happiness.</u>

Next Step: PRAY FOR AND LOVE YOUR ENEMIES!

Matthew 5:43-45. *"You have heard that it was said, 'You shall love your neighbor and hate your enemy.'*

44 But I say to you, love your enemies, bless those who curse you, do good to those who hate you, and pray for those who spitefully use you and persecute you, 45 that you may be sons of your Father in heaven; for He makes His sun rise on the evil and on the good, and sends rain on the just and on the unjust.

Next Step: Communicate Truth to ALL in Leadership!

Be in communication with State and National representatives. Request the return to, the restoration of America!

Next Step: Communicate Truth to ALL in the Region & our America, our Nation!

Continue to invest daily time with fellow believers and non-believers to pass on the truth to all who have ears to hear and eyes to see! Remember, Christ remained with the people in the region. He did not limit himself to those who 'already knew the truth'. He demonstrated the truth! We are to do the same and more!

The LORD has promised a way for us to live, to worship and pray together to redeem our lives, to restore the years and the land! Will you join in repentance prayer?

Now that the truth is revealed to you, I pray we will come together, willing to participants in repenting for all that was done against the people and the land so we will live in truth, speak truth, regain the blessings upon our lives, our families, our communities and the blessed ONE NATION UNDER GOD known as America!

Anything else we need to do?

Yes.

Strengthen our faith and our belief and give credit to the only living LORD over our lives who grants us hope and a future!

Where we are weak, He is strong!

II Corinthians 13:7-9.

Now I pray to GOD that you do no evil, not that we should appear approved, but that you should do what is honorable, though we may seem disqualified. **8** For we can do nothing against the truth, but for the truth. **9** For we are glad when we are weak and you are strong. And this also we pray, that you may be made complete.

Divine Protection:

Include divine protection within daily prayers.

Our Father provides divine protection for us!

In David Barton's *America's Godly Heritage* book, he includes a quote by an Indian Chief whose tribe is not identified, a Chief who traveled to meet with George Washington in 1770, 15 years after the battle in 1755 which would have been the end of Washington's life.

The Chief confirmed he gave the battle strategy to take out all of the officers because then the troops would scatter.

The Chief stated his rifle never missed and he knew that he shot Washington 17 times.

The Chief instructed his men to stop shooting Washington because he was protected by the Great Spirit.

On page 16, the Chief confirms, *I have traveled a long and weary path that I might see the young warrior of the great battle. [I am] come to pay homage to the man who is the particular favorite of Heaven and who [can] never die in battle.*

To preserve our American Heritage, pray for divine protection!

It is obvious GOD has placed our President Donald J Trump in the top leadership position due to all of the revelation, the wisdom given to him each day from our LORD, along with the grace of GOD to handle extreme attacks while bringing forth truth which many across America did not know as truth! Many have threatened him.

Praying We The People will gather together NOW as a body of believers with full faith and pray specifically for GOD's divine protection for America, for our President and for ALL in leadership who are operating in truth! May all be revealed to us which is NOT truth so ALL who are given the leadership opportunity will seek truth and serve the people in truth!

AMEN ... OUR GOD IS A FAITHFUL KING!

Personal Note 'Just Between Us'

Additional delays have taken place due to the in-depth questions from the editors, after I experienced a 'once in a lifetime situation'.

A man's car rear-ended the car donated to my ministry while he was speeding in a construction zone, after we narrowed to one lane of traffic. The hit was so hard, his new(er?) car was dead at the scene while I personally experienced divine protection, again!

My car stopped 'in place'. Clearly angels were holding my car in place! My car did not hit the construction crew working within a couple of feet of the traffic, any equipment or any other vehicles! Grateful to GOD for His divine protection in my life, often!

This moment in time became the first time I have ever been a driver in an accident in my entire driving career. Yes, due to being raised on a farm it's been a few decades!

Before I realized it, days were consumed with calls & appointments, facts which were completely unrelated to this book.

The auto accident was on July 19.

The mid-August release date became a serious challenge!

When the release date was bypassed even though the LORD confirmed the urgency to provide the information prior to the August 21 eclipse, a sign to believers & non-believers of GOD causing movement of the sun from West to East vs. East to West.

I've repented for my focus shifting to other details because this information is critical and the days we are living in are the most unique and unusual days in the history of the believers living on planet Earth!

The two September release dates were bypassed due to the editors asking so many questions! They wanted me to insert everything our Father has shown me during this phase of the journey. However, a 500 page book was not the plan nor was it my desire to withhold anything from you due to the critical status of our lives, our nation of America and Israel.

It was a frustrating moment when the book release was pushed back to the end of September, after the miraculous expression of historic constellations over Jerusalem on September 23. Trusting, still, these facts will be a timely read for you and it will provide the depth of truth which will help you identify the areas of repentance for our lives, our families, our regions, states, and our America!

The ancient and current roots are not being dealt with prior to the most significant days unfolding within the High Holy Days through the days in October, the Feast of Tabernacles. The Signs and Wonders in the Heavens from the eclipse on August 21 continuing through the Holy Days in September, especially on September 23, signs in the heavens which have not existed in this structure at any other time in the history of planet Earth. Amazing days!

The moment I realized another delay in the release date was being scheduled it was so frustrating, I immediately shared the levels of frustration with my hostess. She was in the middle of her prayer time and bible study in the living room.

When I returned to the bedroom, a piece of plain paper with a picture of Jesus was in the middle of the bed.

It was 11:30 PM. No other guests were in the house. I returned to the living room and showed the picture to my hostess. She was surprised. She said she could easily confirm it was not something in the house because she had not seen the picture before.

The next day, I was sharing details about the picture appearing the night before, 'out of nowhere', with a few people at Channel 49 in Augusta. James Murray was listening to the details. He said he purchased a painting similar to the picture about 20-30 years ago.

He offered to bring the painting to the studio the next day.

The two are similar! The copy provided supernaturally is the one I prefer because His hair is thicker on top and His face and body are significantly thinner!

When the painting was shared, our Father immediately confirmed the painting was purchased 25 years ago.

This fact is significant as summarized in **Chapter 3 Significance of Albany Georgia to America.** Our LORD confirmed many connections which He orchestrated *For The Sake Of America* 25 years ago.

It just took 'humans' a while to catch up with what our Father was asking us to do!

Exactly as the photos appear above, the statue at the Guido Gardens near Metter, Georgia, confirms how Jesus appeared to Michael Guido often vs. the image within the paintings of Jesus we have viewed 'over time'.

While my friend Heather was touring the gardens, she was prompted to send me a photo of the statue of Jesus.

When I thanked Heather for the photo and told her about GOD's insistence that I focus upon the lost tribes, she loaned me a copy of *The Apocrypha.*

History about The Apocrypha.

As of the 1611 version of the King James bible, The Apocrypha was still included within a completely separate section from the Old Testament which was located in about the middle of the bible.

In 1825, the British and Foreign Bible Society decided to remove The Apocrypha from the bible. Interesting that the Pilgrims brought the true and complete bible to America in 1620, the land the Native Americans knew as the promised land was removed from British rule when it became a nation in 1776. Then, the removal of The Apocrypha from the bible by the British and Foreign Bible Society in 1825 became what we aligned with as truth.

It is evident within the repeating pattern from ancient to current history, it becomes painfully obvious there are many layers to repent for in each of our lives and that is merely the beginning of the repentance required to 'set the captives' free.

Perry Stone shared a special word during his interview on Channel 49 and I was privileged to be in the audience that day. He also identified the requirement for repentance for the same three levels identified within scripture:

- ○ Individual,
- ○ Regional,
- ○ National.

Hope For Believers

Hope For America

Pray for America. Pray for Georgia, North & South Carolina.

Pray for all of the states in the nation. Pray for all leaders.

Pray for unity within the body of Christ, in our homes, our communities, and all States across the nation until America heals.

THANK the LORD that His hand is upon us and all plans of the enemy are thwarted, for the LORD's hand to be upon America and His favor to be evident and shared in the testimonies from ALL of the people within the Body of Christ in these days.

Remember the word is the truth and the LORD's promise is based upon our willingness to stand firm in faith!

Deep in our heart where Christ resides, we do know there is ONLY ONE WAY, ONE TRUTH, ONLY ONE NAME ABOVE ALL NAMES, ONLY ONE SAVIOR Jesus Christ of Nazareth, the ONLY Son of the Father, our LORD Almighty, the ONLY LIVING LORD.

LORD thank you for your promise!

Thank You for providing the angelic vortexes over Macon, Georgia and Moravian Falls, North Carolina 'For The Sake Of America'!

Grateful to know Your hand is upon us and You will never leave us or forsake us!Thank you for providing Your truth in Your word and through Your prophets so we will be prepared to march with You before the SONrise!

Amen (Hebrew meaning, Our GOD is a Faithful KING!)

Bill and Gwen Morford shared a special gift, *Fulfillment of Prophecy, The Life Story of Eliezer Ben-Yehuda*. Main quote: *The two things without which the Jews will not be a nation: The Land and the Language.*

He spent the rest of his life learning and sharing the Hebrew language. What will we do for the rest of our lives?

To live from glory to glory, it is important to comprehend that our Savior, Jesus Christ, the Messiah, as confirmed in **John 17:22**, gave us the glory that we would be one, unite together 'In One Accord' as He and the Father are one. He gave us this truth, while He was with us! Blessings upon you until the next ONE MORE TIME* our LORD brings us together!

Sheila

Email: hisbest4usorders@gmail.com

Ephesians 2:19-22 *We are no longer foreigners and aliens, but fellow citizens... members of GOD's household, built on the foundation of the apostles and prophets, with Christ Jesus himself as the chief cornerstone. In Him the whole building is joined together and rises to become a holy temple in the LORD. And in Him you too are being built together to become a dwelling in which GOD lives by His Spirit.*

II Corinthians 12:14-15. (a) *"Now, I am ready to visit you...what I want is not your possessions but you...So I will very gladly spend for you everything I have and expend myself as well."*

II Corinthians 13:11-14. *Aim for perfection ... be of one mind, live in peace, and the GOD of love and peace will be with you. May the grace of the LORD Jesus Christ, and the love of GOD, and the fellowship of the Holy Spirit be with you all.*

* While in Ghana, West Africa for the coronation of a King, Bishop Duncan William's worship team sang a simple verse: ONE MORE TIME, ONE MORE TIME, HE HAS ALLOWED US TO COME TOGETHER ONE MORE TIME, and by the third time they shared this verse, pointing to each other, then, to each of us on the platform and then, to each of the participants speaking at least 13 Afrikaans dialects and nine foreign languages, there was not a dry eye in the house!

Research

1. *The Ancient Book of Enoch* by Ken Johnson

2. *The Apocrypha* by Edgar J Goodspeed

3. *One New Man Bible* translated from the Hebrew Manuscripts by Bill Morford

4. *One New Man Bible Companion* by Bill Morford

5. *Fulfillment of Prophecy, The Life Story of Eliezer Ben-Yehuda 1858-1922*

6. *Original Intent* by David Barton

7. *America's Godly Heritage* by David Barton

Ten Commandments in Paleo Hebrew, 500 BC

Preserved by Cherokee, Found near Los Lunas, New Mexico

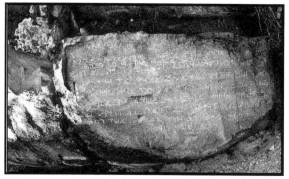

Facts shared by: Steven Collins

http://www.stevenmcollins.com/html/decalogue_stone.html

Artifacts Preserved by New Mexico Epigraphic Society

Douglas Jones, President, New Mexico Epigraphic Society

PO Box 50007, Albuquerque, New Mexico 87181-0007

Books Authored by Sheila Holm

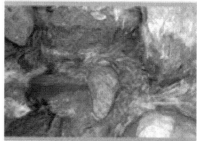

A WAKE UP CALL: IT'S
RESTORATION TIME!

MYSTERIES REVEALED: HOW AND WHEN
THE CHURCH WAS DECEIVED AND WHAT
IS REQUIRED FOR FULL RESTORATION.

SHEILA HOLM

IN SEARCH OF
WIGGLESWORTH

A JOURNEY WHICH SPEAKS TO THE
VERY CORE OF WHAT IT MEANS TO BE A
TRUE BROTHER AND SISTER IN CHRIST!

SHEILA HOLM

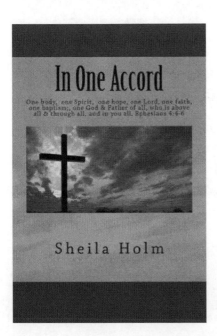

In One Accord

One body, one Spirit, one hope, one Lord, one faith,
one baptism; one God & Father of all, who is above
all & through all, and in you all. Ephesians 4:4-6

Sheila Holm

A PECULIAR
PEOPLE

A holy nation,
a peculiar people.

We are not ashamed of the Gospel of Jesus Christ!!!

DISCIPLESHIP OF PECULIAR
PEOPLE BY PECULIAR PEOPLE

SHEILA HOLM

ALWAYS SPEAK LIFE

For the eyes of the Lord are on the righteous, and His ears are open to their prayers ... 1 Peter 3:12

SHEILA HOLM

CHRISTMAS

Mysteries Uncovered & Revealed: Truth Regarding the Birth of The Messiah, Hidden Since 300 AD

SHEILA HOLM

FOR THE SAKE OF AMERICA

America is in Trouble The Root Problems and the Promises of the LORD are Revealed For The Sake Of America!

SHEILA HOLM

Releasing soon

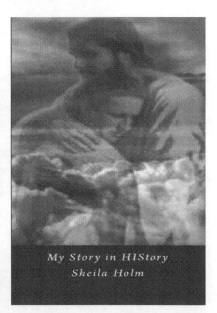

Nation Restoration

Published in 2014

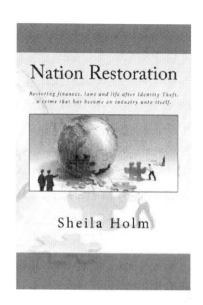

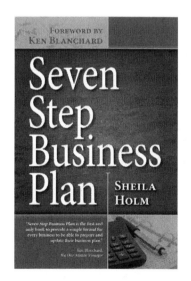

Seven Step Business Plan

Published, 2007

Latin America edition:

Spanish Language

Published, 2009

ACKNOWLEDGMENTS

AFRICA

Ghana, West Africa

Pastor Sam,

"Truly, GOD has sent you to us with a strong word for our church."

Pastor Charles,

"It blesses my soul to hear of your faith & see the fruit of the ministry."

Johannesburg, South Africa

Pastor Jhanni,

"GOD is doing a good work through you and I pray with you and our church."

Coronation Ceremony

AMERICA

Bishop George Dallas McKinney, California

"Sheila is GOD's ambassador to encourage Christians, especially pastors, throughout the US, Africa, Australia and Europe. Without sponsors or any visible means of support, she has traveled the world sustained by the faithfulness of GOD.

Dr. Jan Franklin, Georgia

"Thank you God for answering my prayers by sending Your apostle to (the region) to unite the believers ... "

Prophetess Nancy Haney, Alaska

"God has never given me this before. I see circles and circles and circles ... you drink and you draw from one circle to the other, and that's what you do, you drink and draw and you bring these circles together ... Pulling many groups together. All these groups need each other ... He can use you for you have ears to hear and you hear His deep truth. You are filtering what is nonsense and what is real ... because you have been in that circle, and because of what you say they are going to merge. It is going to expand, become bigger than you could imagine."

Pastor, Host of "Praise the Lord", TBN,

"...The fruit of the ministry is evident in your testimony..."

Man of God (Georgia), Requesting to be Discipled while attending the coronation of a King in Africa, Georgia

"…at my age, it is hard to believe I am learning so much in these few days about what I did not know…realizing what it is to know that I know how it is to live within God's word each day. Will you consider discipling me?"

International Prophet,

"You have remained steadfast to God's plan and God will continue to send you   forth for His plan and purpose to be fulfilled, and for the thousands who have not knelt…"

President, Christian Publishing Company

"Only God could orchestrate such a grand plan…"

Prayer Director, International Prayer Center

"God is opening many doors for you…"

Christian Publisher, "God has given you a powerful voice and a sweet spirit…"

Pastor, Southern California

"God is raising you up and sending you forth to many nations…"

International Apostle

"God is doing a mighty work through you, for His righteousness precedes you, showers over you and follows you as a mighty wake. May it continue for each of your days..."

Prophetic Prayer Partner, Minnesota

"Only God could walk you through these days... accomplish so much through you, in the midst of your daily situations, the many blessings shared during each of your travels will continue to shower blessings upon each of the many households around the world..."

AUSTRALIA

Four Square Gospel Church, Aboriginal Cultural Center

Pastor Rex, "**GOD blessed us through your preaching on Easter Sunday. We will never forget that you were in our midst ... GOD brought new people to Jesus today and we thank GOD for what He has done because you answered His call.**"

Newcastle, New South Wales, Australia

Pastor Mark, "**...the staff and business leaders heard the message of Personal and Professional Life Management this week, so we are blessed you agreed to preach the word to our church this morning.**"

Prayer Team Meeting "**We know now how we will we be able to continue this mighty work when you are not in our midst...**"

ENGLAND

London, England

Pastor Vincent, Glory House, East London, "***...the honor is ours this Easter Sunday.***"

Associate Pastor, "***The Glory of our GOD Almighty shines upon you and through you in your speaking and your actions...we give Him praise.***"

Protocol Team,

"GOD has mightily blessed us by sending you into our midst."

Pastor Arnold,

"You have blessed the people of this congregation, and in His wisdom and timing, may He bring you back into our midst again, very soon."

Pastor, West London,

"We rejoice with you in hearing and seeing the mighty things GOD is doing."

Pastor, South London, "**Our GOD is evidenced in your life and your speaking, while we continue to thank GOD for the work He is doing through you…**"

High Commissioner, Kingdom of Tonga, serving in the Embassy in London, England; Ambassador Akosita, "**GOD's timing is always right…for you to be with us, prior to the Economic Summit, to meet and pray with us…**"

Sunderland, England

Anglican, Former Church of Pastor Smith Wigglesworth

Pastor Day, "**I thank GOD for sending you to our church this morning, for serving communion to me, and for renewing and restoring me for the call upon my life.**"

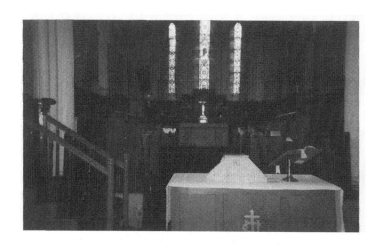

Kingdom of TONGA

Pastor Isileli Taukolo, **"Our board and business leaders were fasting and praying and GOD confirmed He was sending someone to us. We are deeply touched by the message GOD sent to us, through you."**

195

Minister of Finance, Tasi, **"Our meeting was an answer to my prayers, and I thank you for providing the seminar for our senior staff members, and meeting with them individually for prayer and coaching."**

Government Office, **"Thank you for speaking today and for staying and praying with us."**

Interpreter, Sela

About the Author

The LORD fulfills upon His promises within the scriptures. He has equipped and trained Sheila while He:

- Places her feet on the soil of each continent,
- Sends her forth without an extra coin or tunic,
- Arranges flights and accommodations in each nation,
- Introduces her before she arrives,
- Lifts her up and encourages her,
- Seats her before governors and kings,
- Fills her as an empty vessel,
- Shares His wisdom and word of knowledge,
- Blesses and heals the people in her path,
- Comforts & re-encourages her to encourage pastors, prophets, apostles, believers, teachers & evangelists,

- Touches people individually in conferences/multitude,

- Speaks through her with power and authority,

- Takes people into gift of laughter when she preaches,

- Addresses situations the body of Christ is facing,

- Unites the people in the region,

- Confirms His word through her with each prayer & message shared,

- Speaks through her so people hear His words in their own language, especially when the translators also experience the gift of laughter and stop translating,

- Directs her path to <u>speak life</u> into each situation whether GOD sends people to her to be re-encouraged or he asks her to pray with a pastor, the church, or someone in a store or a restaurant, etc.

Vision and word *For The Sake Of America* were given to internationally recognized prophets. They were not able to be 'boots on ground' in Georgia so they shared the facts with people they trusted. Then, the vision and word were released to Sheila because she agreed to remain and fulfill upon the assignment after she traveled across country to Georgia for three weeks in October 2013. The third message from the man who received the vision and word from Bob Jones activated Sheila to proceed with the book. Now, the LORD has provided 'deeper truth' in *For The Sake Of America II.*

Sheila was not aware of the LORD's plan to extend her time to three years or that He would reveal such deep truth to her *For the Sake of America!*

Now, the LORD has extended in Georgia for another year while the 'deeper truth' of the ancient and current roots were being revealed to her, one layer at a time.

However, the LORD confirmed in a specific vision that He sent her to Georgia because she asked for the assignment.

Since Georgia was not part of her conversations with the LORD she was a bit surprised until the LORD reminded her of her own words each time she witnessed the flow of the body of Christ in other nations He sent her to around the world. She hoped the LORD would send someone to bring the truth to the body of Christ in America.

When the LORD reminded her of her heart's desire, she realized in that moment He sent her to Georgia to be available during this critical time in our nation for His purpose, plan and promise to be made known to the people.

The LORD promises once the Ancient and Current Roots Are Revealed, Repentance of the Deeper Truth is Required. Then, the LORD's Blessings Will Flow As A Restoration Flood *For The Sake Of America!*

GOD has taken Sheila around the world, church to church, business to business, nation to nation, set her before governors and kings without an extra coin or tunic.

Many confirm she walks in the five-fold ministry. She does not use a title because GOD does the work while He sends her as an apostle and prophet, and He orchestrates all arrangements for her to preach, teach, and evangelize.

People attending the conferences often say her segments are like watching someone walk out of the bible, share for a while and then, go right back in the bible, aka continue upon her journey in HIStory.

Made in the USA
Las Vegas, NV
24 March 2023

69636735R00111